The Christian Woman

Written by

Loretta Bernard
Jean Boatman
Catherine Chambers
Nancy Dilworth
Judy Keating
Sandra Myer

Karen Myers
Evangeline Rodenbush
Georgia Smelser
Barbara Westberg
Anne Wilkins

This book is designed for personal or group study.

The cover illustration, "I Will Do It," was painted by
Michael Dudash and is inspired by John 14:14,
"If ye shall ask anything in my name, I will do it."
It is available through Ladies Ministries,
e-mail ladies@upci.org.

WORD AFLAME PRESS
pentecostalpublishing.com

Word Aflame Elective Series

Alive in the Spirit
Bible Doctrines—Foundation of the Church
The Bible—Its Origin and Use
Building Family Relationships
The Christian Man
The Christian Parent
The Christian Woman
The Christian Youth
Facing the Issues
Financial Planning for Successful Living
Friendship, Courtship, and Marriage
The Holy Spirit
Life's Choices
A Look at Pentecostal Worship
A Look at Stewardship
Meet the United Pentecostal Church International
Purpose at Sunset
Salvation—Key to Eternal Life
Spiritual Growth and Maturity
Spiritual Leadership and Successful Soulwinning
Strategy for Life for Singles and Young Adults
Values That Last
WHY? A Study of Christian Standards
Your New Life

Pentecostal Digital Reference Library
Volume 4—Word Aflame Elective Series

EDITORIAL STAFF

Robin Johnston. . . . . Editor in Chief
P. D. Buford. . . . . Associate Editor

United Pentecostal Church International

©1989 by the United Pentecostal Church International,
Hazelwood, Missouri. All rights reserved.
Reprint History: 1991, 1992, 1995, 1997, 2000, 2004, 2008, 2010, 2011, 2012, 2014
ISBN 1-56722-042-8

Contents

Chapter   **Page**

Message to Ladies 4

Foreword 5

1. I Am a Woman 7
2. The Divine Institution 19
3. Heirs Together 31
4. To Mothers with Love 43
5. The Working Woman 55
6. Personal Relationships 66
7. Morality 79
8. From Failure to Success 91
9. Putting Your Best Face Forward 103
10. Your Crowning Glory 114
11. Teaching Principles and Standards 126
12. Come to My House 137
13. You and Your World 149

Message to Ladies

GWYN OAKES
General Ladies Ministries President
United Pentecostal Church

The Christian Woman deals with the problems women of this day face in a stimulating and thought-provoking manner and also summarizes dilemmas so common to women in every dispensation.

Women of today are an echo of the women of Bible times. Human nature remains very much the same as centuries come and go. "For all that is in the world, the lust of the flesh, and the lust of the eyes, and the pride of life . . ." (I John 2:16). So we deal with never-changing impulses in an ever-changing world. How wonderful to know the Word of God is contemporary to today's problems.

Because God is no respecter of persons, He uses women as well as men to accomplish His ministry in a world of need. Men and nations are influenced by the qualities of women, and the old adage is as true today as ever: "The hand that rocks the cradle rules the world." Women were, and are, intimately associated with the unfolding purpose of God.

If humanity is to be reached with the saving message of Jesus Christ, it is imperative that today's women be enlightened and spiritually aware. With the sound advice found in the pages of this book, today's Christian woman can see herself as she is—a vital, thinking individual with a responsibility to bear a message of hope and light to a sin-cursed and weary world.

Foreword

LINDA GLEASON
General Ladies Ministries Secretary
United Pentecostal Church

One of the great challenges to a twenty-first century woman is to be a Christian. As the highest calling on earth, it is better than fortune or fame, it is greater than beauty, and it is more noble than high position. The wise man summed it up with these words: "Favour is deceitful, and beauty is vain: but a woman that feareth the LORD, she shall be praised" (Proverbs 31:30).

Women in our society have attained amazing achievements in education, professional life, and politics. For this we are undoubtedly thankful. It seems women have broken out of the box and reached above and beyond anything imaginable by our female ancestors! However, in the reaching, the achieving, the accomplishing, and the successes, we are still mandated by the Word of God to maintain our place as Christian women.

The Christian Woman comes to you from accomplished ladies who have retained their God-given female integrity amidst life's success. The wisdom you glean from their writings comes from experience and not just head knowledge. These ladies have walked through the good times as well as the bad. They understand the joy of achievement, yet many of them have traveled the road of disappointment and deep grief. They bring decades of life's insights and understanding that come only with the living!

The Christian Woman is adaptable. It can be used as teaching material in many different venues such as Sunday school, ladies meetings, and classes for new believers. Every woman of God would be blessed and challenged by reading this book.

It is an honor to be personally acquainted with several of the writers of *The Christian Woman*. I esteem these women of God very highly, having watched their lives of faithful service to the Lord for many years. They have influenced my life; they have set an example to follow. These ladies have done an excellent job of outlining the roles of Christian women. That, perhaps, is why *The Christian Woman* is one of the very popular books in the Word Aflame Elective Series.

Open your heart as you open the pages of *The Christian Woman*, and you will receive blessing, instruction, and inspiration as you walk your personal path of a modern-day Christian woman!

I Am a Woman

And the rib, which the LORD God had taken from man, made he a woman, and brought her unto the man.

Genesis 2:22

Start with the Scriptures

Genesis 1:26; 3:16
Numbers 26:33; 27:1-11
Judges 1:12-15
Proverbs 31:10-31
I Timothy 2:15

In typology, the woman is the type of the church and Christ is the Bridegroom (Ephesians 5:24). In contrast to molding Adam from dust, God *made* or *constructed* Eve from a rib. They were both of the same substance. When Christ died, out of His side flowed both water and blood; by His death the church was purchased (Acts 20:28). Adam, in reference to Eve, stated, "She is bone of my bones and flesh of my flesh." Likewise, Christ considers the church as the "members of His body." Adam and Eve were different, but they were to become as one, to cleave together.

When two pieces of wood are glued together, they "cleave together." The bonded section is stronger than the two individual pieces of wood. When an attempt is made to separate the pieces, the wood will splinter before the bond is broken. "What therefore God hath joined together, let not man put asunder" (Matthew 19:6).

It is impossible to walk away from a marriage unsplintered, or as two whole pieces. A Christian woman should recognize that separation from her husband is not the solution when differences arise, but rather she should seek reconciliation.

Woman, the Help Meet

The term *help meet* means a "helper corresponding to him, a reflection in a mirror." Eve was therefore part of Adam and his aide. The Scriptures explain, "A virtuous woman is a crown to her husband" (Proverbs 12:4). Adam was not complete without his "crown." "The woman is the glory of the man" (I Corinthians 11:7).

The Christian woman endeavors to help her husband keep Christ as the center of his life, or to find Christ if he is unsaved. There are so many pressures in life today until it is easy for legitimate pleasures and jobs to be placed first. A great responsibility is placed on the woman to help keep the house running smoothly.

Church Characteristics and God's Expectations of Women

God designed woman with her unique sensitivity, looking into the future of what He wanted His church to be! The Christian woman is to have the characteristics of the true church in her emotional and spiritual makeup. She must allow the basic, pure nature God originally created in her and restored to her in the new birth to flow. She is to be caring, sensitive, humble, and modest, and she must strive toward perfection in these areas.

From this foundation, we realize God created woman with qualities He wanted in His church. The church is expected to have a relationship, a bond with God that is inseparable. God wanted to save souls for eternity so much that He gave His life. Women, as part of the church, are responsible to be a vital part of His plan. They should not center their lives around everyday chores any more than a man should center his life around his occupation. There must be time to work for God! Simply attending church helps keep them saved and inspired, but what are they doing to further His kingdom? They should consider whether they are helping God as much as they are helping their husbands and themselves to secure a future.

Physically, a Woman

Peter described the woman as the "weaker vessel," frail and delicate in contrast to man and, perhaps, more easily deceived (I Peter 3:7).

Women come in all sizes—small, medium, large, and extra large. The Christian woman should accept herself and keep her body within her proper weight range. Normal, active, healthy, Spirit-filled Christian women should have temperance concerning their weight.

Femininity, the Christian Value System

Changing cultural values may influence the world, but Christians have a value system derived from the Word of God. The world is gravitating at a high speed toward a repeat of Romans 1:24-32, which cites homosexuality (lesbianism) as a culmination of apostasy. Christian women consciously clash with the world's lack of values to uphold true feminine traits.

God's expectation is that sexes outwardly be differentiated in three ways: by their hair, dress, and actions (I Corinthians 11:5-15; Deuteronomy 22:5 with I Corinthians 6:9). The Scriptures reveal that the man who is "effeminate" is not going to heaven. This term means unmanly, like a female. Evidently, the focus is not on the sex act since fornication, adultery and homosexuality are also listed in this same verse of Scripture. Since it applies to feminine acting men, it would seem to apply to mannish type women also.

Some examples of masculine women would be shown in a person's manner of walking, talking, sitting, and conduct. For a Christian woman it would also involve avoiding that which traditionally pertains to a man; likewise her hairstyle and mannerisms should be feminine. A lady's clothes should be feminine. For this reason a critical eye must be given to the latest fads and fashions.

Today, many women are in managerial positions. Even if they are empowered with authority by virtue of position, they must maintain their femininity and not be mannish in the execution of their authority.

Being a Lady Is More Than Being a Woman

Christian ladies care about their appearance inside and outside of the home. They are conscious of the fact that they represent the church. They are concerned about being modest and moderate concerning clothes. Trendy, seductive, or mannish clothing is not for them. Manners and courtesy are a part of their traits.

The training of children includes helping them to adjust to any type of life to which God would call them. Christian ladies want their children to be adaptable and not scornful of those who have more or fewer material possessions than they have. They wish to teach their children correct priorities in life that begin with getting the gospel out to the world, even at a personal sacrifice!

Emotionally, a Lady

"Scream it out. Allow yourself to express all of your hurts and anger to the person who has upset you," is the attitude in the world today. This theme, though, is not for the Christian woman.

The tongue controls the entire body (James 3:2-9). What we say, whether negative or positive, will have a strong bearing on what we become.

Regardless of basic temperaments (sanguine, phlegmatic, choleric, or melancholy), if the fruit of the Spirit is evident, then a woman is under control. If she is not under control, it is a sign God is not the Lord in her life. It is not that she suppresses her basic temperament, but that God has mastered and is ruling her heart.

Nature is like an air-expanded balloon. If it is suppressed, it will become distorted or burst. Likewise, if our nature is suppressed, it will take revenge. Christians do not live a life of suppression, but rather they have been born again. They do not obey God's laws because of legalism, but they live a life of service emanating from their new nature. The Holy Ghost must be in total control.

Natural Barriers

There are natural barriers between women and men. Two aspects of these barriers are conversation and touching. Sometimes there are things that are discussed of a personal nature that pertain to one sex that should not be discussed when people of the opposite sex are present who are non-family members. This does not mean it is vulgar in context. For example, the menstrual cycle and other female-related subjects should not be publicly discussed. If they are, a barrier is broken and the gate is opened to violate other avenues of intimacy. The world uses sexually insinuating phrases and jokes and some of these have even crept in among some Christians. Are we ladies in this respect? What has happened to the blush of embarrassment?

"Keep in touch" is a popular topic from phone companies to psychologists. However, touching can lead to satanic traps.

The author of The *Myth of the Greener Grass*, J. Allan Petersen, gave some illustrations that involved the ministry and touch. One illustration was about a young woman who hugged the pastor after he baptized her. This impropriety was the beginning of something that later caused his downfall. Another example cited was of two couples who were best friends. The wife of one couple was in the hospital and the man of the other couple paid a ministerial call. She held his hand and told him she had been in love with him for over two years. This sparked a feeling that led to his downfall.

We are incapable of knowing if there is a conflict going on inside of someone we touch. How do we know if we are causing someone to have feelings that should not be associated with us? As real ladies, we need to be careful concerning who and how we touch. By using words and formal handshakes to express appreciation to non-family males, we can leave the touching out. Otherwise barriers are broken and gates are opened for temptation.

We need to ask ourselves if we are keeping these natural barriers, thereby keeping ourselves. We are not an isolated island; we do influence others. If we have or our church has gotten into the "touch" fad, perhaps we can be influential in reversing the trend. Everyone knows there is something to the touch. It is good, valid, and needed, but with the wrong peole it is catastrophic.

Physical Problems Affect Emotions

The endocrine (gland) cycle affects different *hormones* (Greek: "excite or stir up") by secretions produced that go directly into the bloodstream. The hormones which these glands send through the blood to various parts of the body act like messengers. They do not actually create, but rather they tell certain processes to speed up or slow down, encouraging or discouraging them. They influence mental, emotional, and physiological functions. This includes at least fifteen hormones among which the most commonly known are insulin, adrenaline, estrogen, and androgen. It also includes such glands as thyroid, adrenal (by kidneys) and gonads (sex glands). If one of these glands is not working properly, it can unbalance others.

If a person is irritable, has insomnia, fatigue, and is abnormally moody, she should check it out. Predicting feelings and moods with charts to determine if these problems come from a physical source can be of assistance. As a Christian lady, one must be able to deal with emotional mood swings.

Christians should not become dependent on tranquilizers and other medications that put them in a daze! After investigation, if it is determined we do not have a physical problem, we must not allow depression, obsessions, or moods to control our minds. Emotions should work for us, not against us.

What God Expects of a Woman

The model woman of Proverbs 31:10-31 is given to show what God anticipates of a woman. The word *virtuous* means "strong in mental and moral qualities." Let us not give all our qualities to a secular job. Rather, let us give our best to God.

The humanist concept is for the woman to bring in extra income so that families can have a better lifestyle. The wife who chooses full employment outside the home places herself and her family at a spiritual disadvantage. In day-care centers children are given role models nine to ten hours a day who are often not Christian. Are Christian women sacrificing their children for "nicer things"?

God wants a woman to have character and morality, to be industrious, and to be a person in whom her husband can have confidence. Women have many talents among which is the ability to manage and plan while being prudent and dependable. This is a full-time job. Certainly this lifestyle is in contrast to that of many modern women. They have no time to do God's work, but have plenty of credit cards and time to use them. They cannot get their housework done, dinner cooked on time, or their children under subjection. They boast that they cannot cook well and constantly are on their way to fast-food places. With the help of God, the Christian lady can determine to get her family and home under control, even if she must work outside the home to provide for the family.

Spiritually, a Christian

Spiritually, women must be strong! Old Testament women claimed their possessions and what was right in the sight of God regardless of the "norm." Deborah was a God-called prophetess and judge in Israel.

Commanded of God, she summoned Barak to lead an attack against Sisera, the commander of the confederate Canaanite forces. Barak consented to go on the condition she accompany him. Even though she was a woman, if it would take her going and keeping in touch with God for him to go, she would go.

She was a prophetess and a judge of Israel and in a position of esteem as a leader! This position did not make her haughty. The tone of the Scriptures does not indicate she thought it was "beyond the call of duty." Her life centered around God, His commands, and His plans. Her focus was not on how she could use her position. God gave her strength and courage and the battle was won (Judges 4:4-24).

Jael, a Kenite's wife, was by her tent. She saw Sisera, the enemy, fleeing. She went out to meet him and urged him to come to her tent. She gave him milk and covered him with a mantle. He demanded she stand outside and if anyone were to inquire if there was a man in her tent she was to answer, "No." Sisera, being weary, fell asleep. She took a nail of the tent and a hammer and drove the nail into his temple. The enemy of Israel died; thus God delivered the enemy into the hands of a woman! A woman met the need! Special emotions and great strength were demanded of her and she did it.

There are times when God anoints women to be used in various ways. However, they cannot succumb to being "super spiritual" women who dominate and are bossy, which is not even a good attribute in men. The woman's adorning is still a meek and quiet spirit (I Peter 3:4).

Boldness and Perseverance in Spirituality

The spiritual lady uses boldness and perseverance in spiritual realms. Zelophehad, a man with five daughters, died in the wilderness. He had no sons.

During this period of Israel's history, only sons could inherit. These five women came before Moses and the elders of Israel pleading for their rights. Moses evidently thought there was merit in the petition and brought it to God. God granted their plea by instituting a new law (Numbers 26:33; 27:1-11; 36:11). They had not yet reached the Promised Land and therefore had not received their inheritance. However, after the death of Moses and the entrance into Canaan, they persevered by reminding Joshua of the new law of inheritance for daughters. They were insistent from the beginning until the physical land was theirs (Joshua 17:3-4).

Achsah, the daughter of Caleb, had recently married and was on her way to her new home. She asked her husband to request a certain field from her father. While Caleb hesitated, Achsah descended from the donkey. Her father asked her what she wanted. She in essence answered, "Give me land and springs." He then granted the request (Judges 1:13-15).

Christian women are not spiritual parasites to their husbands or to their churches. They can do much in a constructive way to strengthen their church. The world would act as a vacuum to draw Christian women into its clutches. Material things can consume their lives if they allow them to. However, their emphasis should be in travailing prayer. They can set the spiritual tone in their churches by re-evaluating their spiritual lives and by petitioning God to make them spiritually active.

A Christian Lady Never Ashamed

A Christian woman has integrity, principles, and honesty. When she walks into the school with her children, her appearance is different from other mothers. She may go to the office as a single woman, but she is not trying to find someone's husband to seduce. She is not ashamed to give her employer an honest day's work. She does not spread her work out so no one will give her more to do. She does not engage in crude office talk or laugh at the vulgar jokes. Instead, she blushes and walks away. But is she ashamed? Never! A Christian lady still prays before she eats. Her lifestyle is on a different level and she is grateful.

Life's demands in these last days require much of the modern, Christian woman. She sometimes faces the desertion of husband or family members, financial crises, unsaved husband, drugs, wayward children, delusion in Christendom, letting down of biblical standards by others, and a continual spiritual fight to keep precious truths. God has forewarned us that the last days would be like this. What should a woman do? She must gather her strength from God, control her emotions and make them work for her.

The Christian woman should not hide behind the fact that she is a woman when it comes to spiritual things. Today, strength and courage are called for beyond the norms of womanhood. God was not greater to His people in the Old Testament. The successful women of the Old Testament were able to endure and have strength because of what they knew to be right, but yet they were not indwelt by the Holy Spirit. By the Spirit of God dwelling in the Christian lady today, she can be victorious!

Test Your Knowledge

1. What are the three major aspects of a woman?
   (a) She is physically a _____.
   (b) _____ she is a lady.
   (c) _____ she is a Christian.
2. What verses of Scripture give God's expectations of a woman?

3. Are men and women both of the same basic temperament?
4. Under biblical principle, is it agreeable for the woman to pursue her own career to the exclusion of husband and family?

Apply Your Knowledge

Welcome honesty and assess yourself as a woman. You are physically a woman. In action, maintain your femininity as a lady. Spiritually, you need to seek to obtain your spiritual rights and still remain a lady. Assure yourself and keep the basic biblical principles of modesty in clothes and speech. In order to preserve yourself and others, beware of touching. Old Testament illustrations serve to prove that you can do things demanded of you, even more, as today you have the Holy Ghost.

Expand Your Knowledge

Observe different classes of people in the secular world. How do they dress? How do different classes act? (Examples: the professional executive woman will dress so that others will respect her knowledge. Actresses will dress to seduce or to make themselves noticed.) Keep in mind that if God made woman in the image of what He wanted His church to be, then there is a more positive standard of what God expects. Therefore, women need to research and observe the Scriptures more closely and see the characteristics of the church. Christian ladies represent the church. You are physically a woman, emotionally a lady and, with fervor, you must press to your rightful spiritual inheritance with God.

The Divine Institution

2

For this cause shall a man leave his father and mother, and shall be joined unto his wife, and they two shall be one flesh.

Ephesians 5:31

Start with the Scriptures
Genesis 2:7-25
Matthew 19:6-12
Mark 10:2-12
Ephesians 5:22-33
I Corinthians 7:10-16
II Corinthians 6:14
I Peter 3:1-12

"And the LORD God formed man of the dust of the ground, and breathed into his nostrils the breath of life; and man became a living soul. . . . And the LORD God said, It is not good that the man should be alone; I will make him an help meet for him. . . . And the LORD God caused a deep sleep to fall upon Adam, and he slept: and he took one of his ribs, and closed up the flesh instead thereof; and the rib, which the LORD God had taken from man, made he a woman, and brought her unto the man. And Adam said, This is now bone of my bones, and flesh of my flesh: she shall be called Woman, because she was taken out of Man. Therefore shall a man leave his father and his mother, and shall cleave unto his wife: and they shall be one flesh. And they were both naked, the man and his wife, and were not ashamed" (Genesis 2:7, 18, 21-25).

With the declaration that man needs a help meet, God met the need and established the institution of marriage. "What therefore God hath joined together, let not man put asunder" (Matthew 19:6).

What Is Marriage for Anyway?

Marriage in any language, culture, or religion historically is the union of a man and a woman who enter into a covenant relationship to live together for the rest of their lives. This covenant commits them, generally through vows, to be faithful to each other, to bear with one another regardless of the circumstances, and to supply each other's needs for their mutual fulfillment.

Man has an innate need to protect and provide for his wife, to be accepted by her, and to provide leadership for her. Woman has an inborn need for protection and love. God provides for the fulfilling of each of these needs in the marriage relationship. (See Ephesians 5:22-33.)

Marriage is generally expected to produce children and therefore the family is expanded in this happy, caring covenant. A man's responsibility to provide, guide and protect is further enlarged as tender, young lives are added to his care. The greatest challenge and joy in a happy marriage is the successful raising of children who in turn become mature, balanced, responsible, happy adults who will repeat this cycle.

For a Christian, marriage has an added dimension—Jesus Christ. Whereas a marriage involves the union of the body (physical relationship) and soul (mental and emotional relationship), a Christian marriage adds one more dimension to marital cohesiveness, the union of spirit (two people joined together in spiritual communion with Jesus Christ). This makes all the difference in the world in regard to the happiness, success, and longevity of marriage.

The marriage covenant provides one with a close friend and companion for the rest of his or her life. That close relationship definitely strengthens the marriage and gives the individuals added courage to combat a hostile world. It also fulfills the need to share one's innermost personal feelings with another individual without fear of rejection or criticism.

There have always been many opposing forces, many philosophies, and many circumstances fighting against successful marriages. But man did not create the institution, and neither will man destroy it. God created marriage just as surely as He created man and woman who are the participants in this divine institution. If God designed the marriage union, and He did, then God provided the physical, social, and spiritual laws to govern it. Those who defy God's laws are not only working against their Creator but they are insuring their own defeat. This applies in all areas of life. God's laws are immutable. In science, the law of gravity controls. In agriculture, the law of the harvest dominates. In the kingdom of God, the law of righteousness rules. We are no less accountable to God's laws in the institution of marriage than in any other created entity which He controls.

An example of man's, or more precisely, woman's attempt to alter God's design for marriage is the feminist movement of the 70s and 80s. This movement among other things declares that women should function in the role of the provider and leader of the family. This, they claim, would improve society. In reality, where feminists have succeeded in part with their plan, there has been a reported increase in crime, violence, and social disorder. The tranquility they promise their followers has not come to fruition. God will not be mocked. His ways are perfect.

Is Marriage for Love?

The key not only to attaining but to keeping a marriage healthy, growing, happy, and exciting is love. We must have a balanced love for God, which allows and encourages love for our spouse. This love will express itself by adequately meeting the needs of one's partner. Indeed, it focuses on the other person rather than on oneself.

The love necessary to establish the depth God intends for marriage far surpasses the expressions of infatuation which are superficial and temporary. It is much greater than a physical attraction which is often selfish in nature. The love essential for the development of a true "they shall be one" relationship is anchored in total commitment, the fulfilling of a vow. It is an act of the mind and will. It is at times emotional, but it does not rely upon feelings. This kind of love gives for the benefit of another, but it does not diminish if it is not returned.

God expressed this kind of love when He provided His Son for a sacrifice (John 3:16). Jesus expressed this kind of love when He died on Calvary for our sins (Luke 23:34; John 15:13). Jesus said that true disciples would be known by a kind of love that the world does not practice (John 13:35). This is the love that only comes from God; and when a person is filled with God, he will be filled with this kind of love (I John 4:16).

The world knows social love or fellowship love that depends on a return. The world also knows physical love which is self-gratifying. But only born-again believers really know and experience the love of God—that committed, giving, sacrificial love. The Greek language has a special word for it: *agape*. The word "love" is the closest equivalent in English, yet it falls short of fully expressing the ideas of *agape*.

Where Paul said, "Husbands, love your wives, even as Christ also loved the church, and gave himself for it" (Ephesians 5:25) the emphasis is on the fact that Jesus "gave himself for it." When husbands give themselves for their wives and wives give themselves for their husbands, then agape love will be in operation. Marriage will stand any crisis when this love prevails.

Every wife wants health, happiness, security, and spiritual blessings in her marriage. She prays for these things and works for them. However, if these things do not come because of circumstances that befall one or both partners, the marriage commitment must not fail. Agape love must continue because it does not depend on results. It depends on vows that were made. Those vows can be kept when she commits her love to God and receives His love in return. Then as a child of God she exhibits that same love toward her husband.

Some Christians have less difficulty loving their neighbor and even their enemy than they do their husband or wife. Perhaps it requires less commitment. But the wise person will learn to love his or her companion all over again. To do less will hinder their ability to pray and relate to God. (See I Peter 3:1-12.)

Is Marriage for Life?

"And the Pharisees came to him [Jesus], and asked him, Is it lawful for a man to put away his wife? tempting him. And he answered and said unto them, What did Moses command you? And they said, Moses suffered to write a bill of divorcement, and to put her away. And Jesus answered and said unto them, For the hardness of your heart he wrote you this precept. But from the beginning of the creation God made them male and female. For this cause shall a man leave his father and mother, and cleave to his wife; and they twain shall be one flesh. . . . What therefore God hath joined together, let not man put asunder. And in the house his disciples asked him again of the same matter. And he saith unto them, Whosoever shall put away his wife, and marry another, committeth adultery against her. And if a woman shall put away her husband, and be married to another, she committeth adultery" (Mark 10:2-12). (See Romans 7:2-3.)

The alternative to making a marriage work is to live apart, albeit in the same house, or to divorce. A couple living a pretentious life together while not relating to each other puts tremendous stress upon the entire family, and sometimes their trust in God is damaged or destroyed. It is so much better to resolve differences, yield personal rights, and concentrate on making a success of the marriage.

A bad marriage can be a terrible experience. But even the worst situations can be made better by calling upon the resources of God. For every command God gives in His Word there is the power available to carry out that command. As in every difficult situation one faces in life, drawing upon God's power and wisdom is a must. Learning and applying the essential ingredients for a successful marriage will be more than worth the effort. In the words of Dr. James Dobson, noted family counselor, "A good marriage is a lifelong treasure."

There is no excuse for the failure of a Christian marriage where both partners know Jesus Christ. Problems will arise, crises will occur, moments of doubt will have to be overcome, but success, blessing, and contentment are assured if we apply God's principles, pray, and seek His counsel.

Marriages where only one partner is a Christian may experience different degrees of difficulty because of the unbalanced spiritual union with Jesus Christ and His Word. However, even these marriages are promised greater success because of the blessings of God and the sanctification (purifying, cleansing and separation from ungodly influences) of the family that results from God's special care for the believer.

Believers are taught not to marry unbelievers because of the unequal union that results along with the heartaches and conflicts of opposing philosophies. "Be ye not unequally yoked together with unbelievers: for what fellowship hath righteousness with unrighteousness? and what communion hath light with darkness?" (II Corinthians 6:14). Believers who for one reason or another are married to an unbeliever are taught to persevere in the relationship. The purpose of the marriage, in spite of the suffering, is to save by whatever means the believer and to keep any children of the family under God's protection.

Is Divorce Possible?

If the unbeliever refuses to remain in the marriage relationship of a spouse who has become a believer, then the believer is fully free from condemnation. In other words, believers are always compelled by the Scriptures to endeavor to correct whatever problems arise and to make the marriage a viable, lasting relationship. (See I Corinthians 7:14-16.) Why? As an example to other Christians, for the benefit of any children involved and because marriage is an institution where we can best learn to serve God, we make every effort to preserve the union. It is the best and most secure place to overcome our weaknesses and to become mature, adult believers who are striving to become the eternal bride of Christ—the real marriage for which we are preparing.

Paul gave added insight into the responsibilities and purpose of marriage in Ephesians 5:22-33. He likened the love of a man for his wife to the love Christ has for His church. Believers must work toward making their marriages successful and lasting because of the testimony it gives to the unbelievers as well as other believers.

The failure of marriages can be expected in a chaotic, sinful, and humanistic world. There will always be those who do not understand what is involved in making a marriage a success. Some by their own lack of knowledge will destroy the very relationship that they need and desire. There will also be those who deliberately choose not to make the marriage a success. Nonetheless, we must strive to achieve the godly ideal of marriage and to eliminate divorce.

Is Divorce Advisable?

Divorce, although an alternative, is also an invitation to disaster. Poverty is often cited as a cause for marriage breakdowns; however, this claim is faulty. In many, perhaps most cases, divorce thrusts women and children into poverty. In ninety percent of divorce cases the wife receives custody of the children, and she is immediately faced with the full responsibility for all the family's needs. More than one-half of all children who live with only one parent are living in poverty compared with only fifteen percent of the children in the general population, according to the 1986 "Status of the American Family" published by the U.S. Bureau of Census.

In addition to a decrease in income and increase in responsibility, the wife is, in most instances, left with the feelings of abandonment and inadequacy. The children of divorced parents suffer tremendous loss. Rising feelings of guilt, plummeting self-esteem, and economic decline are the most cited consequences. These children also often suffer academically.

Children whose parents divorce around the time they begin school have a tendency to link the divorce with their exit from the home to attend classes. They therefore often dislike school. Lawlessness, drug addiction, and sexual promiscuity with all of its resulting consequences are more prevalent among youth from broken homes. We can ask ourselves the question, "Is divorce advisable?"

The family is God's intended school for teaching values, culture, and faith. The freedom of a nation rests upon strong families. Satan's effectiveness in destroying the marriage and home is manifest throughout the world. Some totalitarian governments in the twentieth century attempted to destroy the family unit to ensure their power upon their nations.

The United States has witnessed an attack upon the family for the past two decades. The laws of the states and the federal government alike have changed. The rights of the family unit, which were once fully protected by the laws of our land, are slowly deteriorating to allow alternative lifestyles of live-in couples and even homosexual marriages. Moreover, the nation is assuming more and more control of the children, sometimes and in some instances interfering with the rights of parents to choose for their education and health as well as methods of discipline.

As the United States lets down the standard of a strong family policy, introducing a policy of no-fault divorce, the nation experiences a rise in the divorce rate. Divorce has apparently become acceptable for any reason.

The church cannot allow itself to let down the standard established by God. At the core of the divorce situation is the philosophy that we as individuals are not responsible for what happens to us. Circumstances are seen as responsible or it is seemingly the other person's fault. Allowing ourselves to believe this lie will open the door to spiritual deterioration.

Although the world may accept divorce as a normal way of life, a natural consequence of a changing idealism, the church must stand firm upon the Word of God. God instituted marriage, and He alone has the right to set the criteria for it. "Therefore shall a man leave his father and his mother, and shall cleave unto his wife: and they shall be one flesh" (Genesis 2:24). (See also Matthew 19:5.) "What therefore God hath joined together, let not man put asunder" (Matthew 19:6).

Is Marriage for Everyone?

Traditionally, ninety-five percent of Americans have chosen to marry at some time in their life. That long-standing norm began changing in the decade of the 80s with ten percent of the population remaining single.

Is it okay to be single? Singleness is an acceptable biblical choice. However, it is evidently not desirable for many people as Jesus related to the disciples in Matthew 19:10-12. We should note that the apostle Paul was single and recommended the single lifestyle. (See I Corinthians 7:7-8.)

Some people are called to a life of singleness by circumstances, others by choice. Mental or physical handicaps preclude marriage for some. Others sense a definite calling upon their lives that prohibits marriage in order to fulfill that calling. In many instances it is simply a matter of a person not finding someone with whom he would desire to spend the rest of his life. It is certainly better to remain single than to marry the wrong individual.

Fear motivates certain young people to avoid marriage. The reports of high percentages of marriages ending in divorce are sobering. Personal experiences of growing up in a broken home or witnessing friends who are unhappy in their marriage can cause even the more optimistic person to fear or at least seriously doubt his ability to have a successful, happy marriage.

Marriage Is God's Divine Plan

Although one should very carefully consider the responsibility and commitment required in marriage, it is not to be avoided because of fear. Marriage is a divine institution established by God for the good of man. "It is not good that the man should be alone" (Genesis 2:18). God would not design such a plan for mankind if there were not within that design the ingredients for the success of His plan. To the fearful, the Scriptures speak, "Trust in the LORD with all thine heart; and lean not unto thine own understanding. In all thy ways acknowledge him, and he shall direct thy paths" (Proverbs 3:5-6).

Marriage is God's divine plan. It is for love and it is for life. It is the responsibility of humanity to search the Scriptures for the principles God intends us to apply to our daily lives in order to work His plan successfully.

Test Your Knowledge

1. Marriage is the union of a man and woman who enter into a _____ relationship.
2. The institution of marriage was established by _____.
3. During the 1970s and 1980s a social force attempting to alter God's design for marriage was the _____ _____.
4. True love must be anchored in _____.
5. _____ is superficial and temporary and is not a lasting emotion upon which to build a marriage.

6. Ephesians 5:25 likens the love a man should have for his wife to _____.
7. "A good marriage is a lifelong _____."
8. More than _____ of all children living with only one parent are living in poverty.
9. The family is God's intended school for teaching _____, _____, and _____.
10. Some people are called to a life of singleness by _____, others by _____.

Apply Your Knowledge

As you reflect upon the scriptural basis of this chapter, you can be thankful for God's divine plan concerning marriage. His way is best. Take time to express this thankfulness to God as well as asking Him for assistance in making your marriage the best that it can be.

Expand Your Knowledge

Carefully research the Scriptures given in this chapter. Then study any additional verses of Scripture that deal with this subject. While doing further study, keep in mind that God's plan for marriage should not be influenced by current customs or practices that are contrary to His Word.

Heirs Together 3

Likewise, ye husbands, dwell with them according to knowledge, giving honour unto the wife, as unto the weaker vessel, and as being heirs together of the grace of life; that your prayers be not hindered.

I Peter 3:7

> **Start with the Scriptures**
>
> I Corinthians 7; 11:8-15
> Ephesians 5:21-33
> I Peter 3:1-7

When God's structure for marriage is mentioned, a warning gong sounds and one word flashes across the minds of women, *submission*. The reaction is similar to saying "sic 'em" to a bull-dog. "Women libbers" characterize the submissive woman as "barefoot, pregnant and in the kitchen." This picture of servitude sends a shudder echoing through offices, clubs, and kitchens and some women arm themselves with banners and amendments.

What is the proper balance between the barefoot, pregnant scullery maid and the pushy, militant demonstrator? Where is the happy medium between the dominated wife and the liberated woman? How can a woman be both a submissive wife and a free individual? What, according to the Scriptures, is the wife's role in marriage?

Some misinterpretation of God's Word comes because we do not correctly translate the variations in word meanings. For example, consider the word *good*. In Luke 18:19 Jesus said, "None is good, save one, that is, God." Yet in Acts 11:24 Barnabas was called "a good man." There is no contradiction here if we understand the different shadings of the word *good*. Only God is perfectly good. Yet man can be good, "having positive or desirable qualities; superior to the average."

As we study God's design for husbands and wives, we will pay special attention to the translation of key words.

The First Woman

Creation, from the vast Milky Way to the minute atom, is well organized and perfectly balanced. *Kosmos*, a Greek word often used in reference to the universe, refers to "a system where order prevails."

At the close of each day of Creation God viewed His well-ordered handiwork and said, "It is good." On the sixth day God formed man and placed him in the garden. Then God said, "It is not good that the man should be alone; I will make him an help meet for him" (Genesis 2:18).

To understand God's order for marriage, we must go back to this passage of primary reference, the first marriage. Man's aloneness was "not good," so God fashioned Eve to be "an help meet for him." The original Hebrew meaning of the key word *help meet* portrays someone who "assists another to reach complete fulfillment." Various translations read: "a helper suitable for him," "a helper correspondent to himself," and "I will make him a helper meet (suitable, adapted, completing) for him."

Eve, fashioned from Adam's rib, was actually the missing piece of his life. She corresponded to him perfectly—physically, mentally, emotionally, in every way. Because of their differences, they completed one another. Adam's strengths made perfect Eve's weaknesses. His weaknesses were covered by her strengths. Each was different, but each was vital to the other. They complemented one another.

God introduced Eve to Adam. Marriage is God's idea, and it is good . . . it is very good.

Adam declared, "This is now bone of my bones, and flesh of my flesh" (Genesis 2:23). As neither Adam nor Eve had parents, the next verse (24) cannot be a quote from Adam: "Therefore shall a man leave his father and his mother, and shall cleave unto his wife: and they shall be one flesh." It is believed this admonition was given by God to Moses when the account of the Creation was written. The importance of this principle was verified by Jesus in Matthew 19:4-6 and by Paul in Ephesians 5:31.

To *cleave to* implies "to stick upon, to glue to, to join one's self to closely." For better, for worse, Adam and Eve were stuck with one another. In the garden or out, it was Eve for Adam, Adam for Eve. There was no running home to "mama."

After the creation of Eve, God again looked at His creation and this time declared it "very good" (Genesis 1:31). Everything was in order. Male and female created in God's image were "heirs together" of this earth and given joint dominion over it. (See Genesis 1:26-31.)

Then sin entered the picture. God commanded Adam, even before the creation of Eve, not to eat of the tree of the knowledge of good and evil. Apparently, Eve received God's instructions through her husband, via God's chain of command. When she disobeyed and ate, she rebelled against both the authority of her husband and God. So part of the curse placed on women was in direct relation to Eve's rejection of Adam's authority: "and thy desire shall be to thy husband, and he shall rule over thee" (Genesis 3:16).

The Hebrew word for *husband* means, "to dominate, to rule or master." A woman who is honest will admit that inside her is a longing for her husband to take control. She wants him to be boss, to set his foot down (occasionally and gently). She has trouble respecting a man who will not be a man. She reaches out and yearns for a husband who will accept responsibilities and make firm decisions.

The Liberated Woman

Yet many women spend their lives denying this inbred desire. The National Organization of Women (NOW) was formed by women (and men) fighting God's system of order for marriage and the family. Supporting "full equality for women in truly equal partnership with men," NOW promotes the adoption of legislation prohibiting discrimination on the basis of sex (the ERA amendment), supporting child-care centers and other innovations to permit women to work while rearing a family, and reappraising laws and mores governing marriage and divorce. NOW also favors abortion.

"Women libbers" proclaim that before a woman can be fulfilled and happy she must have a career and not be "just a housewife." They portray the housewife shackled by dirty dishes, diapers and laundry, a slave to the every whim of husband and children. But consider the plight of the career woman—bound by a clock, a desk and red tape, accountable to supervisor or a board of directors. At least the housewife's supervisor loves her, provides for her, and is concerned about her welfare. The career woman's employer is interested only in her intellect and skills to perform tasks for the company. Let her skills slip a bit and her security is gone.

In her book, *I Am A Woman By God's Design*, Beverly LaHaye says, "The strategy to revolutionize the American society into a socialistic, humanistic nation holds women as the number-one target." Betty Friedan, modern-day mother of the feminist movement, claims that the women's-rights movement is structured for two phases.

The first goal is passing the Equal Rights Amendment. Three states short of this goal, the ERA gasped its last breath in 1979. However, its concept and influence are still with us.

The second phase of the women's liberation movement is "bent on changing every institution in our society to agree with the philosophy of the feminists, including the institutions of marriage, the family, education, the military, religion, and so forth." We find the roots of the women's-rights movement in secular humanism, a religion which worships "self."

In Greek mythology, Narcissus was a youth who pined away in love for his own image in a pool of water and was transformed into the flower that bears his name. *Narcissism* refers to "excessive love of self." A narcissistic woman seeks her rights, is unduly concerned about her physical appearance, and constantly strives to be the center of attention. While this type of woman screams for freedom, she becomes more and more enslaved to self. Serving self only brings frustration and bitterness.

In direct contrast, the Christian woman does not seek her rights, dresses in modest apparel so as not to draw undue attention to the physical, and adorns herself with a meek and quiet spirit. By submitting to God's divine plan of authority, she experiences true liberation which comes only through knowing and obeying truth. (Read John 8:32.) The Christian woman finds true liberty when she serves Christ by serving her husband, her children, and others. In so doing, she finds fulfillment and freedom.

The Dominated Woman

On the opposite side of the pendulum from the liberated woman is the dominated woman. When this woman marries, she erases every idea, opinion and belief from her brain. Then her husband reprograms her to think exactly like he does. If a situation arises which she has not been programmed to handle, she has to wait until he gets home from work to make her decision. She asks him whether to buy five or ten pounds of potatoes. And she threatens the children, "You just wait until your daddy gets home!" How wearisome this woman must be to her husband.

"Barefoot, pregnant and in the kitchen" is wonderful for a season. But there comes a day when a woman needs to put on her shoes and go to town. And her husband does not have to hold her hand when she crosses the street.

God gave women brains the same as He did men. When women refuse to use their minds, they throw away one of God's greatest blessings. Just as God did not make robots out of men, men are not to make robots out of women.

Men view situations practically; women view them emotionally. When husbands and wives are able to discuss matters intelligently, listening to and weighing each opinion, many disastrous mistakes are avoided.

Jesus respected womanhood. He came into this world through the womb of a woman. Many of His friends were women. He ministered to them, and they ministered to Him. The first person He appeared to after His resurrection was a woman.

It has been noted that the more heathenistic a society, the less humane their treatment of women. Christianity gives dignity to women.

The Submissive Wife

Here is where the "flags start flying." But we should take a closer look at the word *submission* in the Word of God.

"Submitting yourselves one to another in the fear of God. Wives, submit yourselves unto your own husbands, as unto the Lord" (Ephesians 5:21-22).

The Greek word for submitting means "to place in an orderly fashion under." When God planned His creation, He instituted order. In the universe, the church, the home, there has to be organization. Someone has to be in control. There has to be a system and a manager or there is chaos.

Jesus Christ is a beautiful example of submission. (Study carefully Philippians 2:6-8.) The Son (flesh) submitted to the will of the Father (Spirit) and became obedient. His submission brought salvation. So a wife's submission can bring salvation to her family (I Corinthians 7:14; I Peter 3:1-2). Submission brought Jesus Christ glory (Philippians 2:8-11) And glory and honor will also come to the wife who submits (Proverbs 31:28-31).

There is also a close connection between submission and service. Happiness simply cannot be found apart from submission and service.

Peter's reminder of how Sarah called Abraham "lord" causes women to cringe. Some women cannot imagine calling their husbands "lord." This word *lord*, however, is another key word.

Lord as used here is translated from the Greek word *kurios*. It was "a title of honor addressed by subordinates to their superiors, or as a courteous appellative in the case of persons closely related; applied to near relatives, to a father, a husband, brother, etc.; as a courteous greeting to a stranger." Sarah used it as a wifely courtesy to her husband. Today we might say, "sir." It conveyed her respect for her husband.

Certainly, a wife should always speak courteously and respectfully to her husband. The apostle Paul wrote, "and the wife see that she reverence her husband" (Ephesians 5:33).

Submission is for husbands, too. (Read I Corinthians 7:4.) Ephesians 5:21 tells us to submit "one to another." Sarah was not a doormat for Abraham. She expressed her views very vocally. And Abraham, at times, submitted to her desires (not always for their good). At one time God even told Abraham to listen to Sarah and do as she asked (Genesis 21:9-13).

When a final decision must be made and husband and wife are not in agreement, the wife should submit. Then the responsibility of the outcome rests on the shoulders of the husband.

Paul presented in Ephesians a beautiful analogy. (Read Ephesians 5:23-33.) Just as Christ is the head of the church, the husband is the head of the wife. Just as Christ loved the church and gave Himself for it, so the husband should love his wife.

Chuck Swindoll, in *Strike the Original Match*, asks two questions. To husbands: "Are you willing to die for your wife?" To wives: "Are you willing to live for your husband?" Husbands are not told to "rule the roost." They are commanded to "love their wives as their own bodies." Wives are commanded to "submit and reverence." For husbands it is a sacrifice of love; for wives it is a service of love. For both, marriage is a daily exercise in unselfishness.

The Wife of the Unbeliever

The question often asked is, Are Christian wives commanded to be submissive to unbelieving husbands?

Peter and Paul gave special instructions to the woman with an unbelieving husband. (Read I Peter 3:1-6 and I Corinthians 7:12-16.)

Peter was writing to some new Christian wives who were zealously trying to convert their husbands. Because of their spiritual superiority, they were having trouble with submission. Peter admonished them to stop preaching to their husbands and start being Christian ladies. Nothing speaks louder than a life.

Wives are to submit unto their husbands "as unto the Lord" (Ephesians 5:22). The wife is to be submissive to her husband, as unto Christ, viewing it as an obedience to Christ, recognizing the husband as representative to her of Christ, the head of the church.

The center of the Christian woman's life should be Jesus Christ. If her life is centered on her husband, whether he is saved or not, something will be lacking in her life. If Christ is the focal point of her life, everything else will balance. She will be able to submit to and respect her husband, even though he is not a Christian.

What if a husband expects his wife to go against her convictions? First, she should consider, "Would submitting cause me to sin?" If so, she must obey God rather than man, for God's authority is above man's. Her submission is to be as "unto the Lord."

But Ephesians 5:24 says the wives are to be subject to their husbands "in every thing." Notice that this passage is also referring to husbands who love their wives as Christ loved the church. Kenneth Wuest, in his *Word Studies in the Greek New Testament*, says, "The words 'in everything' refer to everything in the marriage relation."

But what if the issue involved is not a sin, but something she is uncomfortable doing? The wife should examine her attitude. Does she feel and act rebellious and resentful? Or self-righteous? Has she kindly and clearly explained to her husband her feelings? If so and her attitude is right, yet he still insists that she obey his wishes, what then? Prayer and fasting can change him.

What if she is submissive to him and he takes advantage of her? Alford translates I Peter 3:6, "As long as the believing wives are doing good, they need not be afraid with any sudden terror of the account which their unbelieving husbands may exact from them." The *Amplified Bible* says, "not giving way to hysterical fears or letting anxieties unnerve you." Relax. God is bigger than any man.

The believing wife's responsibility is to submit to her husband "as unto the Lord." She is to put on the ornament of a meek and quiet spirit and stay with her husband. Without a word he can be won to Christ. It may not happen overnight; it may take years. But it can be done!

Heirs Together

"There is neither Jew nor Greek, there is neither bond nor free, there is neither male nor female: for ye are all one in Christ Jesus" (Galatians 3:28).

Under the Hebrew law of inheritance, the property was divided among the sons with a double portion going to the first-born who was responsible for has mother and unwed sisters. Only if there were no sons could the inheritance go to the daughters (Numbers 27:8). Widows and unwed daughters were cared for, but only in extreme circumstances could women receive an inheritance.

Then Jesus Christ came. Under grace women can be partakers of the spiritual inheritance. Husband and wife together in Christ "are joint heirs of the grace (God's unmerited favor) of life" (I Peter 3:7 *Amplified Bible)*. The wife is not merely a recipient of her husband's blessings; she is a partaker of the inheritance.

Spiritually men and women are on equal footing, "heirs together," just as Adam and Eve were before the Fall. But naturally we are still under the curse, contending with the carnal nature. Men have to fight weeds and earn their living by the sweat of their brow. Women suffer in childbirth and are under the rule of their husbands. But being in submission to a man who loves you is not bad—not bad at all.

In God's order for marriage, woman is

> . . . weaker but not less intelligent,
> . . . submissive but not subservient,
> . . . subordinate but not inferior.

"Women libbers" have branded submission as a weak, ugly word. Actually, it is a powerful, beautiful characteristic. "Love [God' love in us] does not insist on its own right or its own way, for it is not self-seeking" (I Corinthians 13:5, *Amplified Bible*). Love makes submission easy.

"Nevertheless, in [the plan of] the Lord and from His point of view woman is not apart from and independent of man, nor is man aloof from and independent of woman; For as woman was made from man, even so man is also born of woman. And all [whether male or female go forth] from God (as their Author)" (I Corinthians 11:11-12, *Amplified Bible*). Man and woman . . . husband and wife . . . heirs together. "And God saw every thing that he had made, and, behold, it was very good" (Genesis 1:31).

Test Your Knowledge

1. Paul compared the relationship of husband and wife to _____ and the _____.
2. Wives are admonished to _____ to their husbands while husbands are admonished to _____ their wives.

3. "Ye shall know the _____, and the _____ shall make you _____."
4. A narcissistic woman is one who _____.
5. The only thing about creation that God said was "not good" was man's _____.
6. Woman is _____ to man but not _____ to him.
7. _____ makes submission easy.
8. Wives are to wear the ornament of a _____ and _____ spirit.
9. _____ addressed her husband Abraham as _____.
10. The unbelieving husband can be a recipient of the blessings of God because of his wife's _____.

Apply Your Knowledge

Check your apparel. Are you wearing the ornament of a "meek and quiet spirit"? If your prayers are not being answered, could it be because you are not being submissive to your husband? What area of this lesson spoke to your heart?

Make a list of three things you can do to improve your marriage and start to work on them today.

Expand Your Knowledge

Study these marriages: Abraham and Sarah; Isaac and Rebekah; Ahab and Jezebel; Mary and Joseph. Consider the role of the wife and the influence her submission (or lack of it) had upon her family. Apply your findings to your life.

To Mothers with Love

4

When I call to rememberance the unfeigned faith that is in thee, which dwelt first in thy grandmother Lois, and thy mother Eunice; and I am persuaded that in thee also.

II Timothy 1:5

Start with the Scriptures

I Samuel 1-2
I Kings 3:16-28
Luke 1:26-38; 23:27-28
Matthew 14:3-11
II Timothy 1:5

Motherhood is a God-given privilege. With every privilege comes a responsibility, and one must give an account to God for that which He has entrusted into his keeping. "For unto whomsoever much is given, of him shall be much required" (Luke 12:48).

A mother is the female parent in God's plan for replenishing the earth. "And God blessed them, and God said unto them, Be fruitful, and multiply, and replenish the earth" (Genesis 1:28).

Implanted deep within the heart of every woman is a desire to fulfill her God-given purpose in life. From earliest childhood, when she cradles a favorite doll in her arms in her childish way and mimics her mother in caring for it, a reflection of God's intentions for her begins to emerge.

Some women face the task of motherhood completely frustrated and unprepared. This need not be. God in His wisdom has allotted nine months for a human life to develop within the womb of its mother, and at the same time He develops a woman to love and care for this precious gift He is entrusting into her keeping.

Next to the love of God, the love of a godly mother is perhaps a child's most precious possession.

Real Mothers—Mothers of the Flesh

Hannah. One of the women who personifies the ideal in motherhood is Hannah. Her story is told in the first two chapters of I Samuel. It tells of her desire for a child and the love and care of a worthy son by a worthy mother.

Hannah, one of the two wives of Elkanah, was barren. She had the love and respect of her beloved husband, but this did not dispel her longing for a child. She loved God with all her heart and believed that He was the Creator of all things. As such, He could convert a barren woman into a productive mother.

Every year she joined Elkanah, Peninnah, his other wife, and their children as they traveled to the Tabernacle in Shiloh. Her heart was deeply grieved because she had no children to bring to the Tabernacle with her. Her most ardent prayer was for a man child.

Eli, the high priest, misunderstood Hannah as she poured out her anguished soul in silent prayer to her Maker. "And she vowed a vow, and said, O LORD of hosts, if thou wilt indeed look on the affliction of thine handmaid, and remember me, and not forget thine handmaid, but wilt give unto thine handmaid a man child, then I will give him unto the LORD all the days of his life, and there shall no rasor come upon his head" (I Samuel 1:11). The uncut hair of Hannah's child would be a sign that he was consecrated to God.

Eli thought she was drunk because her lips moved but her voice was not heard. She assured Eli that she was not drunk but that she was a woman of a sorrowful spirit and had come to lay her petition before the Lord. "Then Eli answered and said, Go in peace: and the God of Israel grant thee thy petition that thou hast asked of him" (I Samuel 1:17).

God heard her earnest prayers and in due time Hannah was blessed with the birth of a son. She called his name Samuel, which means "asked of the Lord."

Hannah did not return to the Tabernacle until Samuel was weaned. She then brought the child to Eli and thus fulfilled her vow to God. As she prayed in the Tabernacle she lifted her voice in praise to the God that had answered her prayers. Although Hannah would miss her first son, she had no fears in leaving him with Eli the high priest. She had placed Samuel in the hands of God, and she knew He would take care of him. Each year her skilled hands fashioned a coat for Samuel and she brought it to him when she came to the Tabernacle to worship God. What a thrill it was to see him grow physically and spiritually.

Hannah gave her child to God and then slipped into the background and became renowned through her son Samuel.

Mary—The Mother of Jesus. Mary was an obscure, but godly, peasant girl chosen by God to bring forth the awaited Messiah into the world. "Now the birth of Jesus Christ was on this wise: When as his mother

Mary was espoused to Joseph, before they came together, she was found with child of the Holy Ghost" (Matthew 1:18).

Espousal among the Hebrews was considered the beginning of a marriage and was as legally binding as marriage itself. It could not be broken except by a bill of divorcement. Thus Joseph was referred to as the husband of Mary during the period of engagement prior to their marriage.

When the angel Gabriel appeared to Mary during this time, she was troubled and frightened at his salutation. He assured her, however, that she had found favor with God and she would be the prophesied virgin chosen to bring forth the promised Son whose name should be called Jesus. "And Mary said, Behold the handmaid of the Lord; be it unto me according to thy word" (Luke 1:38). Mary was completely yielded to God's will for her life.

Joseph was also visited by an angel in a dream, assuring him that Mary had conceived a child by being overshadowed by the Holy Ghost. She had not been unfaithful to him as some would suppose, but she was a chosen vessel for a special task. Thus faithful Joseph took Mary as his beloved wife and together they awaited the birth of Jesus. Tenderly he cared for Mary, shielding her from the treacherous accusations and protecting her on the journey to Bethlehem. Joseph was appointed by God to be her guardian and earthly provider. When there was no room in the inn at Bethlehem, it became his obligation to find a place where the Christ child could be born.

All their doubts and fears disappeared as Mary and Joseph gazed together into the lovely face of Jesus. God's promises had been fulfilled and before them was the child through whom God's covenants would be established.

Mary and Joseph carefully fulfilled all the custom of the law concerning the child Jesus. They brought him to the Temple as a baby. There Simeon and Anna pronounced a blessing, acknowledging Jesus as the promised Messiah.

Again at the age of twelve, Jesus was taken by Mary and Joseph to the Temple in Jerusalem for the Feast of the Passover. There He astounded the learned teachers of that day with His wisdom. The concerned parents returned to the Temple after discovering that Jesus was not among those who were traveling home. They did not fully understand His mission, but in obedience to His earthly parents, Jesus returned home to Nazareth.

Mary and Joseph were chosen for a most unusual and holy mission. If, as tradition suggests, Joseph died when Jesus was in His teens, Mary must have felt the pierce of the sword alone when she stood at the foot of the cross and saw Him crucified. "When Jesus therefore saw his mother, and the disciple standing by, whom he loved, he saith unto his mother, Woman, behold thy son! Then saith he to the disciple, Behold thy mother! And from that hour that disciple took her unto his own home" (John 19:26-27).

The last mention we have of Mary was in the upper room on the Day of Pentecost where she was gathered with the one hundred twenty awaiting the promise of the Holy Ghost. Although she was chosen to be the mother of her Lord, it was still necessary for her to be filled with the Holy Spirit on the Day of Pentecost. Only a Spirit-filled life is acceptable for the kingdom of God. As wonderful as motherhood is, it is not synonymous with salvation.

Eunice and Lois. Timothy the son, Eunice the mother, and Lois the grandmother represented three generations of a New Testament Christian family.

In writing to Timothy, the apostle Paul commended all three in II Timothy 1:5. "When I call to remembrance the unfeigned faith that is in thee, which dwelt first in thy grandmother Lois, and thy mother Eunice; and I am persuaded that in thee also." The definition for *unfeigned* is: "sincere, real, true, genuine."

Timothy's family lived in Lystra. His father was Greek and his mother was Jewish. It is thought that his father died during Timothy's childhood, and Eunice, his mother, worked to provide a living for the family, leaving Grandmother Lois at home to care for young Timothy.

Eunice and Lois were excellent teachers and taught Timothy the truths of God's Word. Paul recognized that Timothy was the recipient of excellent training and would be an excellent companion to him and worker for Christ in the New Testament church. Paul loved Timothy dearly and lovingly referred to him as his dearly beloved son.

Paul knew that the religious faith of Lois and Eunice had been handed down to Timothy. "And that from a child thou hast known the holy scriptures, which are able to make thee wise unto salvation through faith which is in Christ Jesus" (II Timothy 3:15). This is a lasting memorial given to a wonderful grandmother and mother by the apostle Paul. He further admonished Timothy to "continue thou in the things which thou hast learned and hast been assured of, knowing of whom thou hast learned them" (II Timothy 3:14).

Eunice and Lois seem to tell us through the Word that nothing should be more important in a mother's life than the early training of her child. Perhaps if Timothy had not had this early training, he would not have been prepared to travel with Paul in the ministry.

We can imagine the sadness that Eunice and Lois experienced when Timothy left them, but they must also have experienced great joy in their hearts knowing they had trained him well in his formative years. Like Hannah of old when she left Samuel at the Tabernacle in Shiloh, they could relinquish their beloved Timothy and say also, "I have lent him to the LORD; as long as he liveth he shall be lent to the LORD" (I Samuel 1:28).

"Train up a child in the way he should go: and when he is old, he will not depart from it" (Proverbs 22:6).

The Heart of a Mother

When Solomon became king over Israel, he asked the Lord for an understanding heart that he might judge the people and discern between good and bad (I Kings 3:9). The Lord was pleased with Solomon's request and granted him wisdom and riches beyond measure.

Solomon's wisdom was put to the test when two harlots dwelling in the same house came before him pleading their case. Each had given birth to a son three days apart. Like most infants of such a tender age, the babies probably looked very much alike. One child died in the night when the mother laid on it. She quickly and quietly exchanged the dead child for the living child which lay in the other woman's bosom (I Kings 3:20).

In the morning the real mother quickly discovered that the dead child was not her own and her living child was in the arms of the other woman. Thus they laid their petition before Solomon. Who was the rightful mother of the living child? As the women anxiously awaited the king's verdict, he asked that a sword be brought to him so that he could divide the baby and give one-half to each woman (I Kings 3:25).

"Then spake the woman whose the living child was unto the king, for her bowels yearned upon her son, and she said, O my lord, give her the living child, and in no wise slay it. But the other said, Let it be neither mine nor thine, but divide it" (I Kings 3:26). The two mothers by their own words had revealed their identity. King Solomon now knew which was the real mother and gave the living child to her.

It has been said that a man thinks with his mind, but a woman thinks with her heart. Her love for God, her husband and her children is a God-given gift and comes from the depths of her heart.

A Mother's Influence

"As is the mother, so is her daughter" (Ezekiel 16:44).

From earliest childhood, children look to their parents for guidance. Mother is their earliest model and she becomes their example for good or for evil, depending on who is the master of her life. If the Lord is her master, she will reflect His goodness to the lives of her children. On the other hand, if she is the servant of the wicked adversary, her deeds will be motivated by the evil one.

The most striking Bible example of the evil influence of a heartless, determined woman is the story of Herodias and her daughter Salome.

Herodias was the second wife of Herod Antipas. She was descended from a line of wicked people. In her deceitful way she divorced her husband Herod Philip and married his half brother Herod Antipas. To Herodias' first marriage had been born her dancing daughter who had been brought up in the evil atmosphere of the family.

John the Baptist was one who dared to speak against this adulterous marriage to Herod. "For John said unto him, It is not lawful for thee to have her" (Matthew 14:4). Herod would have put John to death but he feared the people, for they looked upon John the Baptist as a prophet. Vindictive Herodias held a bitter hatred for John and desired to have him put to death but was held back by Herod. In her cruel determination to be rid of John, she entered upon a foul scheme to accomplish her purpose.

It was King Herod's birthday and a great celebration feast was held in his honor. Herodias sat back and looked on as her daughter danced before the king according to her plan. Her sensuous dancing so pleased Herod that he promised with an oath to give her whatsoever she would ask up to half of his kingdom. "And she, being before instructed of her mother, said, Give me here John Baptist's head in a charger" (Matthew 14:8).

Salome became her mother's puppet as she danced before Herod. Though he was sorry, because of his oath Herodias had her way. She was the evil influence for both her daughter and her husband, and the instigator of a horrible crime against the man of God.

Mothers have always had great influence upon their children. Great men and leaders have attributed their station in life to the influence of their mothers. May the Pentecostal mothers of today realize their great responsibility in influencing their children to live for God and to obey His statutes.

Mothers in Israel

Just as a natural mother is sensitive to the needs of her children, God has ordained "mothers in Israel" to be sensitive to spiritual needs in the church.

In this troubled generation there are many needs. To minister to the physical needs of the multitudes is a rewarding vocation, but to minister to spiritual needs is even greater when we realize that the souls of men will live forever. We are not saved by works, but good works are a natural outcome of a redeemed soul. Thus women become "mothers in

Israel" in the church of the living God not by necessity but by personal choice. Some women may not be blessed with the privilege of having natural children, but all women may avail themselves of the privilege of being church mothers.

Paul admonished the aged (mature) women in the church to be examples in holiness and to teach the younger women (Titus 2:3-5).

When Jesus was being led away to be crucified, a large company of weeping women followed Him. "But Jesus turning to them said, Daughters of Jerusalem, weep not for me, but weep for yourselves, and for your children" (Luke 23:28). This admonition still stands true for women today.

God is counting on the Christian women of this generation to be concerned "mothers in Israel." This involves a compassionate caring and reaching out for the lost. Many children and young people have no one who really cares for their souls. Christian ladies can recognize needs and in love and mercy reach out to help.

The love of a natural mother for her own children is beautiful, but it must reach beyond her own family and encompass all with whom she comes in contact. Her prayers can reach around the world, though she may never personally travel far from her home. Her talents may be used unselfishly for others and for the cause of Christ. She may be called upon to give one or more of her children to the Lord's service at home or on a foreign mission field. Her labor of love will not go unrewarded and one day she will hear the words "Well done, thou good and faithful servant: thou hast been faithful over a few things, I will make thee ruler over many things: enter thou into the joy of thy lord" (Matthew 25:21).

A Mother's Task

When it comes to a worthwhile task, there is nothing as rewarding as the challenge of motherhood. It can be demanding, tiring, exhausting, unending, but it is also thrilling, satisfying, enjoyable and fulfilling. It deals with life, which is a gift from God and it therefore demands one's best.

Every mother is a businesswoman. Her business is producing honorable men and women from the raw materials that come to her at her child's birth. A mother's business is to be entrusted with impressionable, pliable lives which she tries to direct in the paths of honesty, honor, love and loyalty to God and to others. It has been said that a good mother is the equal of a dozen schoolteachers, a small convention of clergymen, and a score of policemen and judges.

There is an old adage that says, "Men work from dawn 'till the set of sun, but a woman's work is never done."

A mother is a "Jacquelyn-of-all-trades." She is a singer whose hymns crooned at the cradle and sung at the ironing board or the kitchen sink will, like God's goodness and mercy, follow us all the days of our lives. She preaches sermons one can see as well as hear. She is the only Bible some people of the neighborhood ever read, but she reads from the Bible and teaches us to love the Word of God. She is the interpreter who knows the exact meaning of a baby's cry, a boy's anguished yelp, a daughter's sob or a husband's scowl, and she comes on the run with the exact answer.

Mother is a clever magician, changing heaviest drudgery into life's highest privilege. She makes her sons feel and look like heroes and transforms her ordinary daughters into radiant angels by waving a word of praise. With reassuring words she makes childhood worries disappear and with a touch of her hand she changes a child's chaos into calmness. Thank God for godly mothers!

"If we work upon marble, it will perish; if we work on brass, time will efface it; if we rear temples, they will crumble into dust; but if we work on immortal minds, if we imbue them with principles, with the just fear of God and love of our fellowmen, we engrave on those tablets something which will brighten to all eternity"

—Webster.

Test Your Knowledge

1. Why is motherhood a privilege?
2. Why was Hannah misunderstood?
3. How did Mary, the mother of Jesus, accept the announcement of the angel?
4. Who were Timothy's mother and grandmother?
5. How did Solomon prove who was the real mother?
6. Discuss a mother's influence upon her child.
7. What is the obligation of the aged mothers in the church?
8. What is a mother's task?
9. When is a mother's work done?

Apply Your Knowledge

Use the basis of this study to help you become a better mother. If you have no children, concentrate on becoming a better "mother in Israel."

Expand Your Knowledge

Make a personal study of the women of the Bible. "Study to shew thyself approved unto God, a workman that needeth not to be ashamed, rightly dividing the word of truth" (II Timothy 2:15).

The Working Woman 5

Favour is deceitful, and beauty is vain: but a woman that feareth the Lord, she shall be praised. Give her of the fruit of her hands; and let her own works praise her in the gates.
Proverbs 31:30-31

Start with the Scriptures

Proverbs 31:10-31
Acts 16:13-15; 18:1-3, 24-28
I Timothy 5:11-14
Titus 2:5

Working Bible Women

Women working in the general job market are not a new thing, for women have been working outside the home for many centuries. Although the job opportunities were not as diverse in early Bible times as they are now, women found a variety of ways to supply or supplement the family income when the need arose.

If a woman were looking in the "want ad" section of an early "Chronicle," she might have found these job options: midwives, nurses, dyers, spinners, weavers, maids, merchants, perfumers, servants, singers, tentmakers, and harvest workers.

Deborah

Deborah, wife of Lapidoth, was a talented and ambitious working woman (Judges 4, 5). She was a prophetess, judge, poetess, singer, and leader along with being a wife and homemaker.

Deborah spent many hours each week as a judge and counselor, sitting under the palm tree and communicating with the people of Israel as they came to her for advice.

A woman of sound judgment and keen spiritual perception, Deborah led Israel in an attack on Sisera and the Canaanites, who had been harassing Israel for twenty years. After the victory, Deborah and Barak composed and sang a song of praise to the Lord.

Although Deborah's career, or more accurately labeled "calling," was unusual for her day, she had God's approval and support for her lifestyle. If she was criticized for being a "working woman" in her culture, it is not recorded.

Lydia

Lydia was a working woman in New Testament times. She was the first European convert of Paul at Philippi (Acts 16:14-15, 40) and a native of Thyatira. Lydia, a merchant woman, found time in her busy work schedule as a seller of purple (dye and/or cloth) to spend time in prayer meetings and to extend hospitality to Paul and his associates.

It is believed that Lydia, an astute and prestigious businesswoman, was considerably wealthy. Through this, coupled with a commitment to the cause of Christ, she found ways to further the gospel.

Paul and Silas entered Lydia's home, where they were comforted and ministered to after they had been beaten and later released from jail. When in Philippi, Paul and his companions made Lydia's home their headquarters.

Priscilla

Priscilla was another working woman of New Testament times. She and her husband, Aquila, worked together in a "family-owned business" of making tents (Acts 18:1-3). Along with staying busy with their business, this couple kept busy witnessing for Christ and hospitably opening their home to Paul and other gospel workers. Priscilla seemed able to keep a healthy balance with the physical, social, spiritual and mental factors of life.

The Virtuous/Ambitious Woman

In Proverbs 31:10-31 King Lemuel wrote about the wise sayings he learned at his mother's knee. In this passage his mother described an industrious and caring woman who carried an enormous workload. In today's culture this woman might be termed a "superwoman." One wonders how she found time to eat or sleep! To be this productive the woman would likely have had a detailed work plan she followed to the letter. Notice some of her tasks:

- Finding wool and flax and spinning it;
- Working willingly with her hands (variety of chores);
- Bringing imported food from distant lands;
- Rising early before dawn;
- Fixing breakfast for her household;
- Making the day's plans for her girl servants;
- Looking at a field;

- Buying the field;
- Planting a vineyard with her own hands;
- Watching for bargains;
- Helping the poor and needy;
- Preparing her household for winter (clothes and food);
- Making upholstered coverings of tapestry;
- Clothing herself in silk and purple;
- Making linen and selling it;
- Making belts (girdles) and marketing them;
- Making her husband "look good" in the community;
- Speaking with wisdom and kindness;
- Having children and a husband who appreciated her.

If ever anyone deserved the title "working woman," this woman qualified. She was very enterprising, manufacturing and marketing items and bringing food from foreign lands. Although she dressed in silk and purple and had a definite "touch of class," she did not lose touch with the poor and needy. Nor, in her busyness, did she lose touch with her husband and children. They rose up and called her "blessed." Somehow, this Old Testament "superwoman" had it all put together. She kept a healthy balance and kept her priorities straight.

To Work or Not to Work

At the beginning of 1980, well over forty million American women held jobs outside the home. It is now estimated that three-fourths of all married women and two-thirds of all mothers will work outside the home for pay. On an average, a woman in her lifetime will work a total of 22.9 years as opposed to 12 years in 1940.

Despite this increasing trend of working women, there are still many women who choose not to work outside the home. Many of these women are mothers who skimp and save to live on a husband's limited salary, and they even lower their standard of living to be able to stay home with their families. Paul, in Titus 2:5, encouraged women to be "keepers at home."

Very possibly the best years of a mother's life are when her children are growing up. If she is able to stay at home with them, she is there when the baby takes his first step and says his first word. These and other developmental areas of growth provide unforgettable family memories. The working mother often misses many of these special times. Also, the mother's absence during this vital period of the child's development is possibly harmful to the child at least to some degree.

Most of a child's basic life patterns and personality traits are set during early childhood years, and a mother needs to be available and to contribute to the child's needs during these important years. Much of the teaching a child receives is given spontaneously when questions arise and daily situations demand immediate responses. These are the materials from which mother-child bonding is made.

A child needs leisure time with his mother—making cookies together, reading a book, taking a walk, playing in the park, making a craft and other low-key interactions. Childhood should not be a stressful time.

It is in the best interest of children that mothers stay home and care for them, whenever this can be arranged. Even elementary-aged children enjoy the security of having a mother at home when they get out of school so that they will not become "latchkey" children. But whenever it is not possible, the mother will have to cope with the situation and find the best possible baby-sitter or day-care facilities available.

Although it is an ideal situation for the mother to stay at home and rear the children, life is not always ideal. Sometimes the husband is disabled, or a low income must be supplemented in order to exist in a high cost economy, and there are the single parent situations when women must work even though the children are very young. There are many reasons why a woman must work outside the home. When this happens, the woman must not feel guilt-ridden.

When the "to work or not to work" decision comes, first of all, the husband and wife should make it a matter of prayer, asking God's guidance. Spouses should evaluate the situation, discussing the pros and cons. Questions to answer would include: Is it worth the extra money? Will it hinder the family trips and activities? If children are involved, will trustworthy baby-sitters or day-care facilities be available? Will work shifts of spouses conflict? Can a part-time job be sufficient to provide needed financial supplement? When an agreement is made, the next step is to work out a "working together" plan to make the new venture work.

Working Together

When an entire family is dependent on a stay-at-home mom who takes an outside job, a big adjustment must be made by all members.

Whether the woman works from necessity or choice, she will need assistance with household duties. A good way to approach this is for the husband and wife to sit down and make a list of all the tasks to be done each week. Then each spouse alternately can choose tasks he and she will be willing to do. Keep choosing items until the list is depleted. If there are children old enough to help, give them a chance to choose some tasks they can handle. Simple charts can be posted lest someone forget the tasks he has chosen.

Some couples divide tasks compatibly in a simple manner by following their interest areas. Dialogue might go something like this: "If you'll take care of the laundry, I'll do the yard work." "If you'll declutter and dust, I'll do the vacuuming." "If you'll do the cooking, I'll do the dishes."

The woman is referred to in the Bible as "the weaker vessel" (I Peter 3:7). This being true, the husband needs to keep this in mind and not expect her to carry both a forty-hour workweek and the entire load of household chores.

Household chores need not be considered "womanly" by masculine members of the family. The armed forces assign their recruits many "household duties" such as kitchen work, making beds, mopping and other cleaning projects without the stigma of making them feel feminine.

If the budget can afford it, a cleaning person can be employed to come in and do general cleaning. Even two times a month will give the family extra time for family outings or church activities.

Sometimes when parents are unorganized in household management, beds go unmade from one linen change to another, dishes stack high on the drain, dirty clothes stack up in the corners, clutter gathers to the eaves and the kitchen floor is sticky with spills poorly cleaned up. The children in the home generally accept this environment as normal. Chances are better than average that history will repeat itself and they will live in "pig sties" when they grow up and have their own homes—and not be bothered by it at all.

Learning to be an orderly person is a slow process, line upon line and precept upon precept. Parents must be consistent in their teaching and be good role models. Some good guidelines for the family to observe could include: if you make a mess, clean it up; turn it on, turn it off; open it, close it;

get it out, put it back; put it in the laundry basket if it is dirty, if it is clean, hang it up; and pick it up, don't pass it up.

A family must have teamwork to run a household fairly and smoothly. Psychologist James Dobson tells of an incident that involved his parents. Several years ago his parents were awakened one night by a noise in another part of the house. The couple got out of bed and Mr. Dobson went to check out the noise.

In the unlighted room, Mrs. Dobson was not aware that her husband had left the bedroom. Afraid that the "intruder" was headed for their bedroom, Mrs. Dobson closed the bedroom door and held it tightly.

Mr. Dobson, after finding nothing amiss returned and tried to open the bedroom door. His wife, thinking he was the burglar, held the door more tightly. He in turn wondered if the burglar had gotten in the bedroom and was holding the door. When Mr. Dobson finally called out to his wife, she realized it was her own husband on the other side of the door and not a burglar. In a sense, they had become "enemies" in the mix-up.

A family needs to pull together in unity to create a peaceful, well-run home, and not become "enemies" who pull against each other.

Pacing oneself is important. A little discipline used and some tasks done each day of the week will help the weekend not to be so hectic. We have often seen a motorist pass us at a frenzied speed, endangering others in the process, only to be stopped at a signal light and all those he passed catch up with him. This is wasted motion, much like the *Tortoise and the Hare* story. Consistency is a jewel. It pays off.

When a child performs a task, we should not redo a poorly done job. Rather, we ask him to work on it again. If we bail him out each time, he will depend upon us to cover for him on a regular basis. We need to assign tasks equal to the child's age and ability.

Some parents pay children for chores they do, while others prefer not to handle it this way, choosing rather to give a separate allowance not related to work done. Whatever the choice, children do need to assume responsibility at a young age. "It is good for a man that he bear the yoke in his youth" (Lamentations 3:27).

When a family works together in a structured way, more can be accomplished and sizeable blocks of quality time can be amassed to be used in profitable ways to enrich the family.

Priorities

Of the 168 hours in a week, the working woman will spend an average of fifty hours each week away from home with her full-time job. This calculation varies, depending on time spent traveling to and from work and the length of lunch time taken. Each week she will likely spend about fifty hours sleeping, about ten hours eating, several hours at church, time spent chauffeuring children to and from activities (school, neighborhood and church) and many hours spent on household duties.

When all of the hours are tallied for a week's activity, one wonders how a 168-hour week can contain so many activities.

Setting priorities, or putting things in proper order or perspective, is extremely important to the welfare and smooth operation of a family.

Spiritual matters, which include personal devotions, family devotions, church attendance and church work, must be placed high on a family's priority list. However, as important as this part of life is, a working woman must examine her involvement in church activities to see if there is a proper balance with her family life. She does not have to be on every committee to the point of neglecting her family. It is permissible to say "no" sometimes and not overcommit herself to the place where life becomes frustrating and hectic.

In setting priorities, the whole person and his needs must be considered: the spiritual, physical, mental and social factors. When houses are built, blueprints are drawn to guide the builder through each phase of the structure. Nothing is left to happenstance. The builder comes back to the blueprint many times to see if he is still on target. Should we be less concerned about building a solid family structure?

Test Your Knowledge

1. Name some job options available to early Bible women.
2. Besides being a homemaker, what other jobs kept Deborah busy?
3. Did God frown on Deborah's political career?
4. In what business was Lydia involved?
5. In what ways did Lydia minister to Paul and his helpers?
6. In the writings about the virtuous woman in Proverbs, which of her activities impressed you most?
7. On an average, how many years will a modern woman work outside the home in her lifetime?
8. Name some advantages enjoyed by the women who do not work outside the home, but become keepers of the home.
9. List some valid reasons why it is necessary for some women to work outside the home.
10. Discuss ways a family can work together with household duties when both spouses work.

11. Discuss the pros and cons of paying children for the chores they do around the house.
12. List things the working woman needs to give careful attention to when setting priorities in their proper order.

Apply Your Knowledge

Find more references of other working women in the Bible and compare their lifestyles to those listed in this lesson.

Make and display in your home a chart listing the weekly household tasks for which each member of the family is responsible.

As a working woman, examine your priorities to see if there is a balance in the major facets of your life—spiritual, physical, mental, and social. If improvement in specific areas is needed, decide which plan of action to take.

Expand Your Knowledge

Read several books about working women to discover helpful ideas to improve household management and lifestyles of those in the work world. Here are suggestions: *The House that Cleans Itself: Creative Solutions for a Clean and Orderly House in Less Time Than You Can Imagine* by Mindy Starns Clark; *The Messies Manual: A Complete Guide to Bringing Order and Beauty to Your Home* by Sandra Felton; *Busy Woman's Guide to Soulwinning* by Kimberly Sciscoe (available in both book and CD).

6 Personal Relationships

And the LORD God said, It is not good that the man should be alone; I will make him an help meet for him.

Genesis 2:18

Start with the Scriptures
Psalm 16:11
Matthew 6:15; 18:15; 20:26-27
Romans 12:18
Galatians 5:22-23; 6:1
I Corinthians 13
James 5:16
I Peter 5:5

"And the LORD God said, It is not good that the man should be alone; I will make him an help meet for him. . . . And the rib, which the LORD God had taken from man, made he a woman, and brought her unto the man" (Genesis 2:18, 22).

Thus God created the first human relationship—that of husband and wife. As the earth became populated, other relationships developed: parents and children, brothers and sisters, in-laws, masters and servants, co-workers, friends.

The Necessity of Relationships

"No man is an island," John Donne once said. Everyone needs relationships to survive physically as well as mentally.

In 1915 Dr. Henry Dwight Chapin, a New York pediatrician, discovered a disturbing phenomenon as he prepared a report on children's institutions in ten cities. In all but one institution, every infant under two years of age died. They had all been clothed, fed, and taken care of medically and physically. What was causing such an incredible mortality rate?

As this question was being pondered by medical authorities, Dr. Fritz Talbot of Boston shed some light on the subject. While visiting Germany before World War I, he was shown through the wards of the Children's Clinic in Dusseldorf. Seeing an old lady, apparently not a nurse, carrying a baby on her hip, he inquired as to her identity. "That is Old Anna," his guide replied. "When we have done everything we can medically for a baby, and it is still not doing well, we turn it over to Old Anna, and she is always successful."

In the late twenties several hospital pediatricians introduced TLC (Tender Loving Care) into their hospital wards. With a regular regimen of "mothering," the infant mortality rates dropped dramatically.

Pastor Bob McCool, from West Memphis, Arkansas, had a unique experience with his premature twin grandsons. The doctor extended little hope for the babies. They seemed unresponsive as they lay in the intensive care division. However, when Brother McCool went in to visit them, he talked with them and sang to them as if they were normal, healthy infants. Amazingly, the twins responded to his expression of love. Unfortunately, when he left, the babies again became unresponsive.

Although he spent many, many hours with them, he could not be there all the time. Then he decided to make a tape of his singing and talking to be played to the twins when he was unable to visit. Surprisingly, the infants responded to the tape as well. The nurses also told the McCool family that when they played the tape, the other premature infants in surrounding beds responded.

It is an accepted fact that strong relationships are a positive factor in physical health. Recent studies have shown that people who are married or have strong, positive friendships are healthier and live longer than those who do not. Following one study, Dr. S. Leonard Syme, a public health researcher, reported, "People who have a close-knit network of intimate personal ties with other people seem to be able to avoid disease, maintain higher levels of health, and in general, to deal more successfully with life's difficulties."

In his book, *Dr. Dobson Answers Your Questions*, author James Dobson states his belief that lack of strong relationships among women is a major cause of feelings of loneliness. Many years ago when people tended to stay in the community where they were born, "women cooked together, canned together, washed clothes at the creek together, prayed together, went through menopause together, and grew old together. And when a baby was born, aunts and grandmothers and neighbors were there to show the new mother how to diaper and feed and discipline. Great emotional support was provided in this feminine contact." Dr. Dobson believes that ladies who have close friendships with other ladies are less likely to be depressed.

Building Positive Relationships

Relationships range from that of casual acquaintances to intimate friendships. A person may have a number of casual acquaintances but will probably have only a few intimate friends. Yet every intimate friend was once a stranger. What qualities are necessary to develop good relationships?

The Sermon on the Mount contains a wealth of information. Perhaps one of the fundamental verses regarding relationships is the well-known verse sometimes called the Golden Rule: "Therefore all things whatsoever ye would that men should do to you, do ye even so to them: for this is the law and the prophets" (Matthew 7:12).

To study some of the ways a relationship can be developed or enhanced, Galatians 5:22-23 will be used as a guideline. "But the fruit of the Spirit is love, joy, peace, longsuffering, gentleness, goodness, faith, meekness, temperance: against such there is no law."

Love. Who can fully describe love? Books have been written on the subject. Songs have been composed about it. Yet love seems to defy description. Perhaps I Corinthians 13 best summarizes true love. A relationship based on this kind of love would certainly be an enduring one.

One necessary component of a loving relationship is *communication.* A breakdown in communication has been the culprit in many faltering relationships. The Bible instructs us to communicate: "But to do good and to communicate forget not: for with such sacrifices God is well pleased" (Hebrews 13:16).

Communication is sharing joys, hopes, plans, dreams, concerns, sorrows and pain. Communication, by words or by actions, is the vehicle by which all the aspects of the fruit of the Spirit are expressed.

No doubt most of us have experienced the deterioration of a once close relationship which gradually faded over the years. Julia and Alice are examples. For a while after Julia moved, letters and phone calls were frequent. Then they grew further and further apart. Finally, Christmas cards were the only communication during the year. Then one year even that ceased. Without communication, it is difficult to maintain a relationship.

A vital element of communication is *listening*. Listening is as important, if not more important, than speaking. Real listening requires giving up our preoccupation with ourselves and giving undivided attention to the other person.

Communication makes possible another facet of love: *affirmation*. In his book, *The Art of Getting Along With People*, Cecil G. Osborne advised, "Because we are motivated more by our feelings than by facts, you will have better relationships if you make people feel good about themselves." Many people have a lack of self-worth. Sincere praise (not flattery) builds up a person's sense of well-being.

There is a difference between a compliment and flattery. *Flattery* can be defined as "excessive praise given for ulterior motives." A *compliment* is "an expression of appreciation offered with sincerity, with no thought of personal gain." Affirming a person helps to build a positive relationship.

Another important aspect of love is *commitment*. Without commitment, a relationship may dissolve when problems develop. In any relationship it is unlikely that two people will agree on every issue. But if they are committed to the relationship, they will resolve their differences or "agree to disagree—agreeably."

Another vital element of a close relationship, *transparency*, is possible only within the context of love. Usually, a person is willing to be open and express her innermost feelings only in an unthreatening environment where she feels loved and accepted. And without transparency, only a limited relationship is possible. A person who is unwilling to share her feelings and opinions, and even her faults, does not allow others to get to know her.

Of course a person should use wisdom in this respect. A few people will tell their life story to a person they have just met for the first time. However, being too open too soon, divulging intimate facts of one's life, can make the other person feel uncomfortable. Rather than serving to build a relationship, such a conversation may cause the other person to withdraw.

The Bible tells us to confess our faults to one another (James 5:16). Again, one must use wisdom in doing so. Confessing to a gossiping person could spell disaster. A relationship can be destroyed by a lack of *confidentiality*. If something is said in confidence, that information should not be repeated to anyone.

Joy. The second item listed in the fruit of the Spirit is joy. A person with a joyful, optimistic, upbeat attitude will find it easy to make friends. People are attracted to such a person. Many verses of Scripture admonish us to be joyful or to rejoice. "Rejoice evermore" (I Thessalonians 5:16). "In thy presence is fulness of joy" (Psalm 16:11).

An attitude of *gratefulness* is nearly always a companion to joy. Generally, the more grateful a person is, the more joyful she is. And a thankful spirit greatly enhances a relationship. Doing something for a person who does not appreciate it is not very enjoyable. But doing something for someone who appreciates it brings joy to the person who does it. People in a positive, caring relationship enjoy doing things for each other, and they express their appreciation for kindnesses shown. "In every thing give thanks: for this is the will of God in Christ Jesus concerning you" (I Thessalonians 5:18).

Peace. A peaceful person will enjoy more lasting relationships than one who is critical, grumbling, and often angry. "If it be possible, as much as lieth in you, live peaceably with all men" (Romans 12:18). (See also Hebrews 12:14 and Matthew 5:9.) A person who is at peace with herself and with God will most likely have harmonious, peaceful relationships.

In his epistle to the Philippians, Paul wrote, "I beseech Euodias, and beseech Syntyche, that they be of the same mind in the Lord" (Philippians 4:2). Apparently, conflict had arisen between the two women. Paul was pleading for peace and harmony in their relationship. Much more can be accomplished in working together when people are in one mind, one accord, and working toward the same goal.

Longsuffering. Since no one is perfect, patience is necessary to deal with the imperfections of others. The following statement is attributed to Ulrike Ruffer: "Patience is the ability to put up with people you'd like to put down."

In addition to patience, *forgiveness* is necessary. Holding grudges not only harms a relationship but can damage both emotionally and physically the person holding the grudge. If we want to be forgiven by God for our shortcomings, we must be willing to forgive others. "If ye forgive not men their trespasses, neither will your Father forgive your trespasses" (Matthew 6:15).

Longsuffering includes "going the second mile." There may be times in a relationship when one person cannot, or will not, carry her share of the responsibilities. Perhaps she is physically ill and is unable to do so. To keep the relationship intact, the other person must do more than her share to carry the load. In a healthy relationship, each person is willing to "go the extra mile" to help the other.

Gentleness. One of Aesop's fables tells the story of the wind and the sun arguing over which was stronger. They agreed to a contest. Whichever made a particular traveler remove his cloak more quickly would be considered the more powerful. The wind began the contest by directing an Arctic blast at the traveler. However, the stronger the wind blew, the closer the traveler wrapped his cloak about him. Then the sun had his chance. He beamed down on the traveler with a welcome warmth. As the sun shone brighter, the traveler became so warm that he soon removed his cloak. The moral of the story is: "Persuasion is better than force; and . . . the sunshine of a kind and gentle manner will sooner lay open a poor man's heart than all the threatenings and force of blustering authority."

Being gentle requires *sensitivity* to another's feelings. People communicate nonverbally as well as verbally. But one must be observant to pick up these messages.

Goodness. Besides being good, a person should look for the good in others. It is sometimes easier to see the faults in a person than to see her good points. However, maximizing the good points while minimizing the faults of another is conducive to a good relationship.

One aspect of goodness is *sharing.* This includes giving and receiving. Some people are like dried-up sponges. They take and take but rarely give. Their relationships are likely to be short-lived. At the other extreme, some people willingly give but have difficulty receiving. If given a compliment, they will negate it.

Another commendable trait is *serving* others. "I commend unto you Phebe our sister, which is a servant of the church which is at Cenchrea: that ye receive her in the Lord, as becometh saints, and that ye assist her in whatsoever business she hath need of you: for she hath been a succourer of many, and of myself also. Greet Priscilla and Aquila my helpers in Christ Jesus" (Romans 16:1-3).

An inherent characteristic of a good person is *honesty.* Not only should we be honest in our relationships, but we should be honest in communication. Without the quality of honesty, no one would be able to trust us.

After their honeymoon, Bill and Carrie sat down to their first meal in their new home. Carrie had proudly prepared a chicken casserole. Bill found it distasteful, but not wanting to hurt Carrie's feelings, he pretended that he really enjoyed it. Next week, they had the casserole again. In fact, Carrie wanted so much to please Bill that she prepared that particular dish once a week—until one evening Bill suddenly exploded, angrily telling her that he hated that chicken casserole. Carrie was stunned and hurt. Honesty in the beginning would have saved a multitude of bad feelings.

Of course, honesty must often be coupled with *tactfulness*. For instance, if a lady came to church with an atrocious hairstyle, silence would be better than saying to her, "What an ugly hairdo!" If she asked directly, "How do you like my hair?" a tactful response might be, "I liked it better the way you had it Sunday," or "I think it is more becoming when you wear it in a French roll." A person can be honest, yet tactful, in relationships.

Faith. For a relationship to be a strong, lasting one, it must be based on trust. Having faith in a person is believing that she will do what she has promised. It is also believing that she wants what is best for us—that she will not intentionally hurt us.

Meekness. Selfishness has no place in a good relationship. We should think of others and try to build them up rather than trying to impress them with our abilities. Some people feel that they always have to be the winner—whether it be a game or a conversation. However, the Bible teaches that we should have the spirit of submission. "All of you be subject one to another, and be clothed with humility" (I Peter 5:5).

A meek person will have *respect* for others. If she is the leader of a group, she will not feel that she is the only one with worthwhile ideas. She will solicit suggestions from others. Even though she may not always agree with a statement or suggestion, she will respect the other person's opinion.

Another characteristic of a meek person is *courtesy* to others. By thinking of them and putting their needs first, she nurtures a relationship. She shows consideration for them and makes them feel important. She is happy for the accomplishments of others. She is willing to give them honor. As Cecil G. Osborne said in the book previously mentioned, "If you want to get along well with people, don't burst their bubble."

Temperance. "Let your moderation be known unto all men" (Philippians 4:5). Even good qualities can have negative results if they are overdone. For example, serving others is good. But if a lady spends all her time serving others and neglects her own family, that is not wise.

If all the previously stated qualities are in evidence, good relationships should result. However, we should not be alarmed if everyone does not think that we are the greatest. Personalities differ, and we should make allowances for that. Even among Christians there may be personality conflicts.

Dealing With Conflict

A relationship, especially in its early stages, is fragile. Perhaps it can be compared to a tiny baby who needs to be nurtured to survive, grow, and mature. A relationship needs to be nourished to develop into a strong, mature bond.

Enemies of a relationship must be guarded against and destroyed to keep the bond healthy and intact. Some of these foes are discussed here.

Criticism. As a relationship develops, faults may be more easily seen. A critical attitude may then develop. One reason for criticism may be inadequate information. Our knowledge of others, their backgrounds, and circumstances is only partial at best. We may be too quick to form opinions and judge others.

Wrong attitudes can destroy relationships. "Let all bitterness, and wrath, and anger, and clamour, and evil speaking, be put away from you, with all malice" (Ephesians 4:31). "For I fear, lest . . . there be debates, envyings, wraths, strifes, backbitings, whisperings, swellings, tumults" (II Corinthians 12:20). Any one of these attitudes, if allowed to develop, could wreak havoc in a relationship.

Lack of communication may result from the above problems. A person who is criticized may become withdrawn, less transparent, and thus less communicative. This in turn would probably promote more criticism, and the destructive cycle would continue.

When conflicts develop, they must be dealt with if the relationship is to survive. "If thy brother shall trespass against thee, go and tell him his fault between thee and him alone" (Matthew 18:15). Even if the other person is at fault, the responsibility for attempting to restore the relationship is ours.

Prayer should be the first step in restoration. This will help to assure that we will have the right spirit when we go to the person. When confronting someone, we should do so in the spirit of love with the purpose of restoring the relationship, not venting our anger. "Brethren, if a man be overtaken in a fault, ye which are spiritual, restore such an one in the spirit of meekness" (Galatians 6:1). We need to be spiritual ourselves and have the proper attitude and right tone of voice. Anger should have no place in the confrontation. We should go in the spirit of meekness, not with an air of superiority.

During the actual confrontation, we should confess any wrongdoing or wrong attitudes we may be guilty of that might have contributed to the problem. The conflict may not be totally the other person's fault. In discussing our feelings, it is important to make "I" statements rather than "you" statements to avoid being critical. An example of a "you" statement is, "You made me angry when you criticized my idea in front of the whole group." Rephrased in "I" terms, the statement would be, "I felt angry when my idea was criticized in front of the whole group." The latter is a statement of fact rather than a statement of criticism.

After the problem has been discussed, we should make a clear statement as to what we want the other person to do. "In the future, I want you to discuss with me privately any differences of opinion." Even though the confrontation is made properly, the other person still has the power of choice. He can choose to do as he has been asked, or he may refuse to do so. He cannot be forced to comply with the request.

In dealing with differences of opinion, it is important to genuinely respect the opinions and judgments of others. We need to be tolerant of individual differences. The relationship should be more important than one side winning over the other. In matters other than biblical doctrines, there should be a willingness to compromise when necessary for the sake of the relationship. If each party is genuinely concerned about the survival of the relationship, confession and forgiveness will bring about the resolution of the conflict.

To conclude this chapter on relationships, Cecil G. Osborne's statement is appropriate: "Everyone is laboring under some kind of burden. When you reach out with understanding and concern and love, you will be the one most richly rewarded."

Test Your Knowledge

1. Why is communication so important to good relationships?
2. What is the difference between flattery and a compliment?
3. Explain the quality of transparency.
4. What does "going the second mile" mean in reference to relationships?\
5. Define tactfulness and tell why it is important to couple it with honesty.
6. Discuss why trying to change others usually results in failure.
7. What is a major cause of feelings of loneliness among women?
8. Describe the quality of transparency in relationships and tell why it is important.
9. If conflict develops in a relationship, what should a person do?
10. Why is it important in confrontation to make "I" statements rather than "you" statements?

Apply Your Knowledge

Examine three of your closest relationships. Think back to the beginning of each relationship. What caused the relationship to develop? If there are problems or conflicts in the relationships, determine to pray about the matter, then lovingly confront the other person.

Expand Your Knowledge

You may wish to read the books mentioned in this chapter. Another excellent book is *Women Helping Women: A Biblical Guide to Major Issues Women Face* by Elyse Fitzpatrick and Carol Fitzparick.

Morality 7

For ye are bought with a price: therefore glorify God in your body, and in your spirit, which are God's.

I Corinthians 6:20

> **Start with the Scriptures**
> Deuteronomy 5:18; 22:5, 20-22, 30
> Proverbs 6:27-28, 32-33
> Romans 1:24-32
> Hebrews 13:4
> I Corinthians 5:1-13; 6:9-20; 7:1-5
> Galatians 5:19-21
> I Thessalonians 4:1-7
> Revelation 21:8; 22:15

A *U.S. News & World Report* article entitled "The State of American Values" begins with the unsettling observation, "Rarely, if ever, in American history have questions of morality been so troubling for ordinary people."

The writer continues by noting that "the nation's leadership—political, religious, and scholastic—is sharply divided on issues ranging from family values to business ethics to sexual behavior to drug abuse." The writer goes on to say that "every day seems to carry new challenges to old codes of conduct" and that "many people are re-examining their values and searching for guidance." In the same article, Rabbi Robert Hirt of Yeshiva University made the statement, "Morality is more discussed now than it was 10 years ago because people are up in the air. . . . They are looking for anchors."

Our culture is especially adrift regarding that aspect of morality which concerns itself with sexual relationships. Some are suggesting that what was immoral in years gone by is not necessarily so today. Tragically, even many modern religious leaders brazenly proclaim that it is up to the individual to ascertain for himself what is moral and what is not. The "old standards" for moral conduct have been deemed by thousands as outdated, puritanical, meaningless, and even dangerous.

Countless American women have discarded the old rules for the so-called "new morality" or situation ethics. "If it feels good, do it!" some assert. Others argue that anything is acceptable between consenting parties. And some defend their immorality by contending that "everyone is doing it." One coed glibly summed up what seems to be the national sentiment regarding sexual experimentation. "It's perfectly natural," she said.

Today premarital sex is commonplace. Federal statistics indicate that "about half of the women who married during the early 1960s said they had sex before their weddings. Now, more than four-fifths report they had sexual experience. On average, U.S. girls have their first sexual intercourse at age 16, boys at 15½." By the end of their teens, 70% of girls and 80% of boys are sexually active.

And while attitudes toward extramarital sex remain basically negative, the aforementioned article concedes that behavior has changed. Studies in the 1950s and 1960s indicated that men were more likely to have extramarital affairs than women. But a recent Yale University study for *Psychology Today* of 7,500 readers showed that "45 percent of women as well as 45 percent of men said they had cheated on their spouses or longtime lovers."

God's Plan for Sexual Purity

The writer of the *U.S. News & World Report* article stated that "it is not easy to make moral decisions today" and that "in many respects, morality is a moving target." While making moral decisions may not be easy, the Word of God is explicitly clear on the subject of sexuality. It leaves no room for doubt or confusion for even the most casual reader of its pages.

There are standards which do not change from generation to generation. Moral standards are one such example. As we consider these standards, it is imperative to first recognize that moral standards were not established by men, but by God. Cicero, an ancient Roman statesman and philosopher, correctly noted that, "It has always been the conviction of all truly wise that the moral law is not a creation of man's mind, or something that has been discovered by individual people, but it is something eternal according to which the whole world must regulate itself. Its ultimate basis is in God. . . ."

God's Word is emphatic concerning sexual purity. It absolutely condemns premarital and extramarital sexual relationships. Ultimate sexual expression between a man and a woman is to take place only within the bonds of marriage. Gene Getz, in his book *The Measure of a Woman*, stated it well, "A woman's sexual powers are to be definitely restrictive and used exclusively in relationship to her husband. With all other men she is to be discreet and modest. In no way should she deliberately or even naively attract men to herself sexually. To do so is to violate Paul's instructions to be 'pure.'" (See Titus 2:3-5, *New International Version*.)

Terms Defined

According to *Vine's Expository Dictionary of New Testament Words*, the word *fornication*, as used in the Scriptures, denotes any illicit sexual intercourse, including adultery. Today it generally refers to sex between unmarried people, while adultery refers to sex between a married person and someone other than a lawful spouse. Whatever the terminology, sex outside marriage is prohibited.

This prohibition includes what we today call fornication, adultery, incest, and homosexuality. (See Leviticus 18:6-18, 20; 20:10-21; Deuteronomy 22:20-22, 30; Romans 1:24-32; I Corinthians 6:9-18.) All other types of moral sins such as child molesting, cross-dressing, and pornography are also condemned. Actually, anything that encourages lust is forbidden. (See Deuteronomy 22:5; Matthew 5:28; Galatians 5:19-20; I Thessalonians 4:1-7.)

Premarital Sexual Activity

There's no doubt about it. We live in a sex-crazed society. Sex is used to sell just about everything from plane tickets to perfume. Advertisers appeal to natural drives to peddle their wares. Lyrics to popular songs are suggestive, and respectable magazines are becoming increasingly lewd.

Television programs and movies lead women to think that "everyone fools around." *A Ladies Home Journal* article entitled "Teenage Sex" revealed that "the average T.V. viewer sees more than 9,000 scenes of suggested sexual intercourse or innuendo during prime time alone." Yet, even in a morally decadent society, it is possible for a single Christian woman—whatever her age—to live morally pure.

The apostle Paul, speaking within the context of a culture notorious for its immorality, warned the young unmarried pastor Timothy several times in his letters to avoid illicit sexual encounters. He reminded him that he was to be an example of the believers in purity (I Timothy 4:12). He was to treat "the elder women as mothers; the younger as sisters, with all purity" (I Timothy 5:2). Again in the same chapter, Paul repeated his admonition, "Keep thyself pure" (I Timothy 5:22). Then in a second letter to the young man, Paul sternly reminded him to "flee also youthful lusts" (II Timothy 2:22). Although the advice was given to a young man, it is just as good for young ladies today.

Since the Word of the Lord condemns even lustful thoughts, the unmarried should avoid any physical activity that would inflame the passions (Romans 13:13-14; II Corinthians 10:5; Philippians 4:8). Illicit sex is a fire, and those who "play around" with it can expect to get burned (Proverbs 6:27-28). For this reason, necking and petting are taboo. Even engaged couples must exercise self-discipline in the area of physical contact.

To live a clean moral life is not only a commandment but it is also something to be desired. A news article entitled "I Can't Believe I Lived That Way . . . Did Such a Dumb Thing" relates the story of a housewife in her thirties. Known only as Linda, she lectures in classes on family life and health, urging students not to make the same mistake she did. She tells spellbound students about the "mistake" that forever altered her life, and the "one night of irresponsibility" from which she and those she loves never have been able to shake free.

As a young lady of sixteen, her future was bright—until the night she became pregnant by someone she did not even love. She confides to the high schoolers that she "continues to pay a price for her 'mistake.'" She admits that "the price changes as time passes." "At the time," she says, "I thought that it was only a temporary thing, but it wasn't. It lasts a lifetime. I'm still paying . . . and the price gets higher later as I fully recognize the magnitude of the mistake."

She observes that those she loves—her parents, especially—have paid an emotional price too. She concludes by saying, "Kids today like to indulge in 'fun things,' but 'fun' things have their price."

In Linda's case, the price included an unwanted pregnancy, loss of reputation, self-hatred, estrangement from her family, an aborted education, and, ultimately, divorce.

Tragically, Linda is not an isolated case. A *U.S. News & World Report* article, "A Call to Tame the Genie of Teen Sex," stated that every year one million adolescent girls become pregnant and about 400,000 have abortions.

Even immoral women who do not become pregnant have a price to pay. Experts fear that sexually active young women with multiple sex partners are at a greater risk of developing cervical cancer later in life, not to mention the possibility of venereal disease. In addition, premarital impurity often leads to mistrust, loss of respect, and sexual dissatisfaction in marriage. Besides, those who engage in premarital sex are more likely to engage in extramarital sex.

Yes, premarital sex has its price. And when compared to the consequences, it is simply not worth it!

Extramarital Sexual Activity

Stories of torrid love affairs and wife-swapping abound; nevertheless, the Scriptures are plain. Adultery is sin. One of the Ten Commandments states, "Thou shalt not commit adultery" (Exodus 20:14; Deuteronomy 5:18). And in Mark 10:19, Jesus affirmed the commandment. In fact, under the law the penalty for adultery was death in cases involving a married woman (Leviticus 20:10; Deuteronomy 22:22).

Adultery is also included in several lists of the sins of the flesh, and, as such, it brings with it God's judgment.

- "For out of the heart proceed evil thoughts, murders, adulteries, fornications . . . These are the things which defile a man" (Matthew 15:19-20).

- "Be not deceived: neither fornicators, nor idolators, nor adulterers, nor effeminate, nor abusers of themselves with mankind . . . shall inherit the kingdom of God" (I Corinthians 6:9-10).

- "Now the works of the flesh are manifest, which are these; Adultery, fornication, uncleanness, lasciviousness . . . they which do such things shall not inherit the kingdom of God" (Galatians 5:19-21).

Adultery is an especially grievous sexual sin, for it disregards a God-recognized covenant between a man and a woman. And it is particularly destructive because of the violation of mutual trust upon which a marriage is built. Many spouses never fully recover from the betrayal of trust, and many marriages are destroyed. Those marriages that survive are frequently riddled with suspicion, hostility, and bitterness.

The adulterer also receives a blot against his character that can never be fully erased. The wise man stated, "But whoso committeth adultery with a woman lacketh understanding: he that doeth it destroyeth his own soul. A wound and dishonour shall he get; and his reproach shall not be wiped away" (Proverbs 6:32-33). Although God will forgive a truly repentant adulterer, the consequences of adultery are often irreversible.

The warning is clear: "Marriage should be honored by all, and the marriage bed kept pure, for God will judge the adulterer and all the sexually immoral" (Hebrews 13:4, *New International Version*).

Why Moral Purity?

Why moral purity? Although it should be enough to say, "Because the Bible says so," the Word of God itself offers some insight into the reasons why.

First of all, we do not own our bodies. They rightfully belong to God; we are merely stewards of God's possession. The apostle Paul reminded the Corinthians—who, incidentally, were plagued with moral problems—that "ye are not your own. For ye are bought with a price" (I Corinthians 6:19-20). In I Corinthians 6:13, he explained it this way: "Now the body is not for fornication, but for the Lord; and the Lord for the body." (See also verse 15.)

As Spirit-filled believers, our bodies are the temple of the Holy Ghost. The apostle Paul rhetorically asked the saints at Corinth, "What? know ye not that your body is the temple of the Holy Ghost which is in you, which ye have of God, and ye are not your own?" (I Corinthians 6:19). When a Christian woman commits an immoral act, she is actually desecrating the dwelling place of the Holy Ghost.

Thirdly, those who are immoral sin against their own bodies. Although every sin will condemn a man, the apostle Paul made a distinction between sexual sins and other kinds of sins. He warned the Corinthians, "Flee fornication. Every sin that a man doeth is without the body; but he that committeth fornication sinneth against his own body" (I Corinthians 6:18).

Because sexual sins defile the body, women who ignore the warnings of Scripture and engage in illicit activity risk contracting various venereal diseases, some incurable, including herpes and AIDS. AIDS, which just a few years ago was confined to certain high-risk groups, is now a "plague of the mainstream," according to one study. Experts say that only couples who have had a totally monogamous relationship for the past decade are safe from AIDS.

Fourthly, sexual sins violate the sanctity of marriage. When a couple not married to each other commits fornication or adultery, they are joined as one flesh, something God intended only for the marriage relationship. Again the apostle Paul asked, "What? know ye not that he which is joined to an harlot is one body? for two, saith he, shall be one flesh" (I Corinthians 6:16).

Lastly, those who are immoral will experience the wrath of God. Romans 1:24-32 makes it clear that those who are given over to immorality are "worthy of death." And the apostle Paul told the Colossians that those who practiced immorality were "children of disobedience" and that the wrath of God would come upon them (Colossians 3:6). In fact, Sodom and Gommorah are examples of what will happen to those with unrestrained passions (Jude 7).

The Scriptures are plain. Those who engage in illicit sexual acts shall not inherit the kingdom of God (I Corinthians 6:9-10; Galatians 5:19-21; Ephesians 5:3-6). In fact, the apostle John penned a powerful warning to the immoral: "whoremongers . . . shall have their part in the lake which burneth with fire and brimstone: which is the second death" (Revelation 21:8). (See Revelation 22:15.)

God's Plan for Sex in Marriage

When Karen Shedd became engaged, she wrote to her father for advice, saying, "I'd like you to tell me how I can keep him loving me forever." Dr. Charlie W. Shedd, a minister, father, and husband, began writing Karen a series of letters, which were eventually published in a book, *Letters to Karen*.

Many women come to marriage with unfortunate childhood memories, false impressions, guilt, and anxiety, which all need to be worked through. Shedd offers this advice to those for whom sex may at first be less than satisfying: (a) be "honest with each other and (b) 'love one another with a pure heart fervently.'" He explains that a truly happy and satisfactory sex life is "delicate doing and you must love it, work at it, and care enough to make it whatever is natural and good for the two of you."

To experience intimacy at its best, a scriptural understanding of sex and one's conjugal responsibilities is necessary. First, it should be understood that a desire for a wholesome marriage intimacy is not impure, but rather God-sanctioned. The writer of Hebrews 13:4 wrote that "marriage is honorable in all, and the bed undefiled." (See Song of Solomon 1:13-17; 2:3-6; 7:1-13.)

In fact, God created man and woman for the mutual enjoyment of each other—physical and otherwise (Genesis 2:24). Thus contrary to the thinking of some, sex need not have procreation in mind to be permissible. Sex is also a means of expressing love, concern, and unity. It is a means of meeting not only physical needs, but psychological needs as well.

The relationship should be governed by a Christ-like spirit of unselfishness, humility, self-sacrifice, and love. The apostle Paul reminded the Corinthians that "the wife has no longer full rights over her own person, but shares them with her husband. In the same way the husband shares his personal rights with his wife" (I Corinthians 7:4, *J. B. Phillips*).

The apostle Paul also warned against refraining from intimacy for long periods of time. In straightforward language, he wrote, "Do not cheat each other of normal sexual intercourse, unless of course you both decide to abstain temporarily to make special opportunity for fasting and prayer. But afterwards you should resume relations as before, or you will expose yourselves to the obvious temptation of the devil" (I Corinthians 7:5, *J. B. Phillips*).

The Call to Ethical Purity

Godly women should not seek to be sex symbols, but rather symbols of modesty, purity, and all that is good and wholesome. Everything about a Christian woman's life—her actions, her words, her dress and spirit—should reflect the nature of the indwelling Christ. Christian virtues such as honor and trust, decency and order, kindness and respect are as vital as sexual purity. (See Psalm 15; Acts 24:16.)

It is interesting to note that the apostle Paul ended his discussion of sexual purity with the admonition to "glorify God in your body, and in your spirit, which are God's" (I Corinthians 6:20). And he closed his letter to the Thessalonians by saying, "And the very God of peace sanctify you wholly; and I pray God your whole spirit and soul and body be preserved blameless unto the coming of our Lord Jesus Christ" (I Thessalonians 5:23).

When we allow the Lord Jesus Christ to fully possess us, then our lives and spirits will truly reflect His nature; and we will be pure— body, soul, and spirit. And if we heed the call to purity, a blessed promise is ours. Jesus said, "Blessed are the pure in heart: for they shall see God" (Matthew 5:8).

Test Your Knowledge

1. Describe the moral climate of our nation.
2. In a nutshell, summarize God's plan for sexual purity.
3. As used in the Scriptures, what does the word *fornication* denote?

4. Explain why singles should avoid any physical activity that would inflame the passions.
5. Why is adultery an especially grievous sexual sin?
6. Immorality has its price. What is it?
7. List five reasons for moral purity.
8. Explain why a desire for a wholesome marriage intimacy is not impure.
9. Why is it unwise for married couples to refrain from intimacy for long periods of time?
10. Why is it especially important for women to be ethically pure?

Apply Your Knowledge

During personal devotions, determine that you will accept the challenge to lead others back "to an old-fashioned morality, to old-fashioned decency, to old-fashioned purity and sweetness—for the sake of the next generation." (See Titus 2:3-5.)

Expand Your Knowledge

Many excellent books have been written for singles and marrieds alike. Singles might find *Gates and Fences* by Lori Wagner, and *Five Love Languages for Singles* by Gary Chapman helpful.

Married couples might benefit by reading *Love and Respect* and *Cracking the Communication Code* by Emmerson Eggerichs, *Wired that Way* by Martha Littauer, and *Five Love Languages* by Gary Chapman.

From Failure to Success

8

Which in time past was to thee unprofitable, but now profitable to thee and to me.

Philemon 11

> **Start with the Scriptures**
> Psalm 51:3, 12; 143:10
> Matthew 14:24-33; 26:33-35, 69-75
> Luke 15:21-24
> John 21:15-17
> Romans 8:28
> Philippians 3:13
> James 5:16
> I John 2:1

Life is a blend of failures and successes. No one—especially not a child of God—is a total failure. And no one—except the Lord Jesus—is an absolute success.

Charles Swindoll, in his book *Encourage Me*, wryly noted, "Show me the guy who wrote the rules for perfectionism and I'll guarantee he's a nailbiter with a face full of tics . . . whose wife dreads to see him come home. Furthermore, he forfeits the right to be respected because he's either guilty of not admitting he blew it or he has become an expert at cover-up."

Everyone fails at something at some point in his life. We may have failed others, ourselves, or God. Our list of failures may include a failed marriage, an unsuccessful business venture, a ruined career, or a shattered relationship. We may have received a failing grade, been fired, or not achieved a desired goal. Simply put, failure is a fact of life.

Abraham Lincoln's personal history well depicts life's blend of failures and successes and demonstrates triumph in the face of repeated failure. Consider the following chronology.

> 1831 – Failed in business
> 1832 – Defeated for legislature
> 1833 – Again failed in business
> 1834 – Elected to legislature
> 1835 – Sweetheart died
> 1836 – Had nervous breakdown
> 1838 – Defeated for speaker
> 1840 – Defeated for elector
> 1843 – Defeated for Congress
> 1846 – Elected to Congress
> 1848 – Defeated for Congress
> 1855 – Defeated for Senate
> 1856 – Defeated for Vice-President
> 1858 – Defeated for Senate
> 1860 – Elected President

Charles Swindoll, in his book *Starting Over*, aptly observed, "The person who succeeds is not the one who holds back, fearing failure, nor the one who never fails . . . but rather the one who moves on in spite of failure."

A Biblical Example of Failure

The Scriptures are replete with examples of men and women who failed in some area of their lives. In fact, several of the heroes of faith listed in Hebrews

11 are notable ex-failures. We will briefly consider a few of them in the course of our study. At this point, however, we will focus our attention on impulsive Peter, no stranger to "blowing it."

Sinking beneath the waves. During a fierce storm on the Sea of Galilee, the frightened disciples espied a figure walking on the water toward them. Peter, believing the figure to be the Lord, confidently cried out, "Lord, if it be thou, bid me come unto thee on the water" (Matthew 14:28). When Jesus said, "Come," Peter scrambled overboard into the tumult and walked toward Him. The other disciples could have followed suit. Instead, they preferred the security of the boat.

It was not long, however, before Peter took his eyes off Jesus and began to consider the conditions around him. Moments later, terrified by the boisterous wind, he began to sink beneath the raging waves. How foolish he must have looked floundering in the tempest. For a while it looked as though Peter had made his final mistake.

Yet failure oftentimes serves as a springboard to success. Peter had the wonderful experience of Jesus rescuing him from a watery grave and walking him across the waves to the stunned disciples huddled in the boat. One minute Peter was a failure and the next, a one-and-only! Besides the Lord Jesus, Peter is the only man in human history to have walked on water.

Denying his Lord. On another occasion, Peter boasted that regardless of what anyone else did, he would never deny his Lord (Matthew 26:33, 35). He was emphatic even though the Lord had forewarned otherwise. But he did fail his Friend.

When the pressure was applied, all the disciples turned their backs on the Lord, but Peter did not merely run and hide as did the others. Three times he denied knowing the Lord. He even swore.

We can only imagine the torment Peter suffered that night as he fled from the knowing look of his Lord. Perhaps he agonized, "I wonder how much the Lord heard!" He surely berated himself for failing his dearest Friend when He needed him most. And in all likelihood, he browbeat himself for his cowardice and worried whether his credibility would ever be restored.

Regardless of what went through Peter's mind, we know that he found a place of repentance. The experience had dashed his self-reliance and false bravado. He faced himself squarely that night and acknowledged his weakness and fear.

Then instead of allowing the shame of his failure to separate him from the other disciples, Peter joined John to visit the tomb on resurrection morning. Later when an angel appeared to the women, he specifically instructed them, saying, "Tell his disciples and Peter that he goeth before you into Galilee: there shall ye see him" (Mark 16:7). Jesus had not forgotten Peter.

How did Jesus subsequently respond to Peter? After His resurrection—just as He promised—Jesus had a private meeting with Peter (Luke 24:34). What a precious time of reconciliation it must have been. Peter, the man who failed his Friend in His darkest hour, was forgiven and restored.

Then sometime later on the shores of Galilee, Jesus again conversed with Peter, asking him three times, "Simon, son of Jonas, lovest thou me?" (John 21:15-17). Thrice Peter had denied his Lord, and thrice he was given the opportunity to reaffirm his love.

Then the command was given, "Feed my sheep." Peter was restored to a place of leadership in the presence of the other disciples and with them went on to Jerusalem to await the promise of the Father. There on the Day of Pentecost, he became the spokesman of the fledgling church. The man who failed was transformed into a blazing flame by the power of the Holy Ghost!

Reasons for Failure

Why do people fail? While every situation is unique, most failures are the result of violating certain basic principles. If we are to enjoy future success, we must first discover the reasons for past failures. Those who fail to analyze past failures are likely to repeat them.

The reasons for failure are many. While all of the following reasons may not apply to our particular shortcoming, they will provide valuable insight into the nature of failure. Perhaps they will suggest additional reasons to us.

We were out of the will of God. Instead of being on the battlefield when kings went to battle, King David lounged at home. Weakened by idleness and apathy, David fell into adultery. To cover his sin, he arranged the murder of an innocent man (II Samuel 11:1-27). Although God forgave David, his last years of life were marked by the same treachery and violence that he had sown.

We too can make grievous mistakes when we are out of the will of God. Like David, may we in sincerity say, "Teach me to do thy will; for thou art my God" (Psalm 143:10).

We violated a scriptural principle. When we reject or ignore scriptural principles, we set ourselves up for failure. For example, the Word of God teaches that we are not to be unequally yoked together with unbelievers (II Corinthians 6:14). If we choose to disobey, we incur the displeasure of God and at best strain the doors to true happiness and fulfillment. Joshua reminded the Israelites that if they wanted to enjoy success, they were to do according to all that was written in the law of God (Joshua 1:8).

We failed to seek God before making a decision. Joshua failed his people when he "asked not counsel at the mouth of the LORD" concerning the Gibeonites (Joshua 9:14). Because he relied on his own perception, he signed a treaty with a people he should have destroyed, thinking they were strangers from a distant land. We would do well to take Solomon's advice, "Trust in the LORD with all thine heart; and lean not unto thine own understanding. In all thy ways acknowledge him, and he shall direct thy paths" (Proverbs 3:5-6).

We lacked knowledge. Some people have failed simply because they did not have all the facts. Ignorance is not bliss! It can be costly! The Lord said, "My people are destroyed for lack of knowledge" (Hosea 4:6). We must strive to be well informed concerning the Word of God and those things which pertain to daily living.

We did not weigh the consequences of our words or actions. We need to guard against acting before we think! Impulsiveness can be destructive. Sometimes a hasty word or thoughtless deed can destroy a treasured friendship, a good job, or our credibility. Solomon reminded us, "Discretion shall preserve thee" (Proverbs 2:11).

We did not have confidence in the promises of God. Abraham's faith wavered, and he lied when Pharaoh desired Sarah, his wife (Genesis 12:10-20). Isaac repeated his father's mistake when Abimelech developed an interest in Rebekah (Genesis 26:7-11). Had the men possessed confidence in God's promises to them, they would have avoided their lapses of faith. We can take encouragement from the fact that "all the promises of God in him are yea, and in him Amen" (II Corinthians 1:20).

We are motivated by pride. God hates pride. In fact, He even hates a proud look (Proverbs 6:17). Many downfalls are the result of pride. Solomon plainly stated, "Pride goeth before destruction, and an haughty spirit before a fall" (Proverbs 16:18). We must carefully consider our motives before we speak or act.

We got ahead of God. We make some of our biggest mistakes when we get impatient and rush ahead of God. Many Bible characters failed tragically because they did not wait on God. Abraham and Sarah took matters into their own hands regarding the promised son and paid bitterly for their hastiness. Moses slew an Egyptian and hid him in the sand. Thus he had to flee into exile. King Saul, who was instructed to wait for the man of God in Gilgal, got impatient and offered the sacrifice to God himself. His act of disobedience started him on his downward slide. David advised, "Rest in the LORD, and wait patiently for him" (Psalm 37:7).

Sometimes we experience failure through no fault of our own. A malicious individual may deviously destroy a treasured friendship. A jealous co-worker may cause an innocent victim to be fired. An ungodly spouse may break up a marriage to satisfy his own wicked desires. Or a romance may dissolve just because it was never meant to be. In such cases, we must retain our confidence in God. The apostle Paul assured us that "all things work together for good to them that love God, to them who are the called according to his purpose" (Romans 8:28).

Starting Life Anew

"You're finished! It's all over! You may as well give up!" Satan hisses to the soul who has failed. Take heart! Satan is a liar. God specializes in making something beautiful out of shattered lives. As Charles Swindoll wrote in *Starting Over*, "God is the One who builds trophies from the scrap pile . . . who draws His clay from under the bridge . . . who makes clean instruments of beauty from the filthy failures of yesteryear."

The story is told of a renowned violinist who hired a craftsman to make a violin for him. When the violin was completed, the master violinist expectantly drew the bow across the strings, and to the horror of the violin maker, he went into a frenzy. Suddenly he raised the violin above his head and smashed it to pieces on the table. He paid the man and left in a fury.

Sometime later, the master visited the violin maker again. Picking up a violin in the shop, he was impressed by its tone. How it responded to his masterful touch. To his amazement it was the same violin that he had smashed earlier. The violin maker had painstakingly reassembled the pieces of the battered violin and reconstructed it. The breaking and remaking process had produced a quality instrument.

Our great God is not just the Creator; He is also the great re-Creator! He has the ability to take a defective instrument and make it over anew. And as Fanny Crosby put it, "Chords that were broken will vibrate once more."

Common responses to failure include guilt, bitterness, self-condemnation, anxiety, defensiveness, despair, and depression. Many people who have failed are afraid to try again. Some resort to suicide.

So how does one go about starting over? How does one overcome negative responses and start living positively? These suggestions will help.

Face your mistakes! A deep sense of failure can cause serious emotional damage. If not resolved, the memories of past failures become buried deep within the human psyche and eventually manifest themselves in physical ailments, negative attitudes, personality quirks, and poor overall emotional and spiritual health. Failures need to be faced and resolved, not buried. (See Psalm 51:3; Luke 15:21.)

Accept responsibility for your mistakes! We must confront our failures with ruthless honesty before we can experience emotional healing.

Accept God's forgiveness! God loved us while we were yet sinners, and He does not stop loving us when we make a mistake. John reminded us that "if any man sin, we have an advocate with the Father, Jesus Christ the righteous" (I John 2:1). God will forgive us if we come to Him for forgiveness. And when God forgives, He forgets!

Forgive yourself. "I'll never forgive myself for what I did!" some exclaim after they have failed. But if we want to break the shackles of past failures, we must. Besides, when God has forgiven us, it is an affront to Him to withhold forgiveness from ourselves.

Forgive anyone who might have contributed to your failure! Jesus let it be known that He would not forgive us if we withheld forgiveness from others (Mark 11:25-26). Besides, refusal to forgive compounds inner torment (Matthew 18:21-35). On the other hand, forgiveness frees us from the torturous past and enables us to run toward tomorrow.

Get counseling if necessary! Sometimes talking over our mistakes with our pastor or a trusted spiritual friend can help. Others can provide perspective and offer solutions we might not readily see. In fact, James advised, "Confess your faults one to another, and pray one for another, that ye may be healed" (James 5:16).

Get on with it! In *Starting Over* Charles Swindoll wrote, "Sitting there licking your wounds will only result in a bitter aftertaste. Sighs and tears and thoughts of quitting are understandable for the moment but inexcusable for the future. Get up and get on with it! Nothing damages our dignity like stumbling. Nothing destroys our life like lying there in the mud—refusing to stand up and shake it off." He goes on to observe that failures who give up are useless, but failures who get up are priceless.

Is there life after failure? Indeed! In fact, if we do not get bitter, life just might get better than ever.

A man who restores antique cars was once asked, "Are these restored antique cars really as good as they were when they came off the assembly line in Detroit years ago?" "No," he replied, "They're not. They're better!"

Making Life a Success

Just as violating certain principles leads to failure, putting others into practice will help make life a success.

Let go! Saint Joseph's Health Center in St. Louis, Missouri, issued a brochure entitled "Let Go!" which recommended in part, "If you want to be healthy morally, mentally and physically, just let go. Let go of the little annoyances of everyday life, the irritations and the petty vexations that cross your path daily."

It went on to advise, "But the big troubles, the bitter disappointments, the deep wrongs, and the heartbreaking sorrows, tragedies of life, what about them? Why, just let them go, too. Drop them, softly maybe, but surely. Put away all regret and bitterness, and let sorrow be only a softening influence. Yes, let them go, too. And make the most of the future."

Perhaps one of the reasons for the apostle Paul's greatness is that he knew how to "let go" of the past with all its haunting memories. He reflected on himself, saying, "I count not myself to have apprehended: but this one thing I do, forgetting those things which are behind, and reaching forth unto those things which are before, I press toward the mark for the prize of the high calling of God in Christ Jesus" (Philippians 3:13).

Cultivate a sense of joyfulness. Often a cloud of despair hangs heavy over victims of failure. Many are enveloped by the sense that things will not ever work out, that things will not get much better, that there is no way out of the gloom. King David must have felt that way after his moral failure for he cried unto the Lord, "Restore unto me the joy of thy salvation" (Psalm 51:12).

A secret to vibrant living is a joyful heart. The Israelites were reminded that the joy of the Lord was their strength (Nehemiah 8:10). When we lose our joy, not only is our disposition sullied, but also our ability to resist sin is diminished. Thus we invite additional failures into our lives. We would do well to lay ahold of the promise of "beauty for ashes, the oil of joy for mourning, the garment of praise for the spirit of heaviness" (Isaiah 61:3).

Develop a healthy sense of self-worth. Low self-esteem can be described as a sense of inadequacy and inferiority. It is a nagging inner voice that berates, "You're no good! You always mess things up!" And nothing increases one's sense of worthlessness more than failure. In fact, some who fail may conclude that they are not worthy to be a child of God or even to live.

Jesus said, "Thou shalt love thy neighbour as thyself" (Matthew 19:19). How can we truly love others when we despise ourselves? To be a good wife, a good mother, a good friend, we must first recognize our own worth. A healthy self-esteem will free us to accept God's love in spite of our faults and enable us with confidence to reach out and share that love with others—others who have failed. (See Galatians 6:1.)

Yes, there really is life after failure—abundant life! Failure need not be the incapacitating experience it all too often is. It can be the launching pad into a glorious tomorrow. It is up to us!

We who were at one time unprofitable to God and others, can be a vessel of value once again!

Test Your Knowledge

1. What two times did Peter's faith fail?
2. What was the response of Jesus to Peter's failures?
3. How did Peter respond to his own failures?
4. What are some reasons that people fail?
5. If we fail through no fault of our own, what should our response be?
6. What are some common responses to personal failure?
7. How do we go about picking up the pieces after we have failed?
8. What are three principles for making life a success?

Apply Your Knowledge

As painful as it might be, make a list of the failures in your life. Analyze each one to discover reasons for the failure. List ways you can use the failures as stepping-stones to future success.

Expand Your Knowledge

Feel you are a failure? Read the nineteen testimonies of overcomers in *This Is Life and I Need Answers* by Ladies Ministries. Also, for an ongoing study of this subject, consider reading *Help Me Heal* by Lynda Allison Doty, and *Let's Go Down to the Potter's House* by Joanne Putnam.

These books are available through the Pentecostal Publishing House, 8855 Dunn Road, Hazelwood, MO 63042-2299 (*www.pentecostalpublishing.com* and 866-819-7667).

Putting Your Best Face Forward

But let it be the hidden man of the heart, in that which is not corruptible, even the ornament of a meek and quiet spirit, which is in the sight of God of great price.

I Peter 3:4

Start with the Scriptures
I Samuel 25:14-35
I Kings 21:7-15
II Kings 9:3-35
Psalm 45:13; 149:4
Proverbs 7:9-27
Ezekiel 23:40
I Timothy 2:15
I Peter 3:1-8

Believe It Or Not, You Are Making an Impression

How we look sends a message to the world, whether we intend to or not. Before we ever open our mouth to witness, we have already *testified* by our appearance. It is our first presentation of the Lord to the world. Our appearance is judged by people who will never see our home, our church, our church attendance records, our tithing envelope, or our prayer closet.

In our society, the way we look has become a way of instant evaluation. Is it not true that we involuntarily react to what we see with our eyes—physical appearance? Whether this is good or bad is not the issue. The fact remains that one of the first and strongest messages we send to others is our appearance. How we, and ultimately our God, are received is often dependent on whether this message is positive or negative.

It has been said that it takes eleven positives to overcome one negative. If our first impression to our world is negative due to a sloppy, unkempt appearance, we must then find eleven positive ways to impress others before they will ever listen to our testimony about the Lord.

How many times have we heard, "When I first met you I thought. . ."? Those were people who lingered around us long enough to learn differently, but what about those who are turned off immediately and never learn anything better about us or our God? We may never have a second chance to make a good impression.

Our appearance is especially important because it is connected to our effective witnessing. We want others to see us at our best because we represent Jesus Christ. We must be aware that people outside the church see us in a different light than we see ourselves.

It is a shame when the words unkempt, dowdy, sloppy, and unattractive are thought to be synonymous with Christian appearance. Some are convinced that to be Christian one has to be stuffy, eccentric, unhuman, unattractive and fifty years out-of-date in appearance. Such is supposed to impress others that we are being holy and humble when in reality it is possibly self-righteousness and ego on display and at its worst. The Pharisees thought they were impressing others by not washing their face, not combing their hair, and wearing a sad face so everyone would know they were fasting—that is, being "spiritual." Jesus called them hypocrites. (See Matthew 6:16.) We can never show our Christianity or spirituality by how ungroomed or unattractive we make ourselves.

Eugenia Price in her book, *Woman To Woman*, says it so well: "We all need to remember, as Christians, that we not only 'present our bodies' unto the Lord, we present them to those who don't yet know Him, too. If you offend that person's finer senses, you may slam the door of the kingdom in his or her face."

Is It Biblical To Look Attractive?

First the question can be asked, "Does God love beautiful things?" One has only to look at a beautiful sunset, a majestic mountain, trees changing color in autumn, snow-covered landscapes of winter, a delicate, fragrant flower, or the stars in the heavens to understand how God feels about beauty. In Ecclesiastes 3:11 the wise king wrote, "He hath made every thing beautiful in his time."

Are we not also part of God's creation? It is therefore logical to believe that the master Creator would have each of His children at their best in every area of their lives, including how we look. He is interested in the total person, and that certainly includes our appearance. Our bodies are a temple of His Spirit and God has always been concerned as to the appearance of the temples where His Spirit dwells.

In Genesis 3:21 is recorded God making the first clothing for Adam and Eve. Evidently, He was concerned about what His creation wore. It is also reasonable to assume that He could make clothing as beautiful as He could make a flower. In Exodus 28 are God's specific instructions to Moses as to the color, design, fabric, and decorations for the priests' garment for "glory and beauty." The virtuous woman in Proverbs 31 made herself attractive with clothing.

The Bible speaks of the beauty of women in a positive, not negative, way. Even God Himself was pleased with His creation of Eve. Considering the rest of His creation, we can assume that Eve was a beautiful woman. Sarah was so beautiful that even at sixty years of age her husband, Abraham, feared the king would have him killed to obtain her.

The Bible lets us know that others, like Rebekah, Rachel, and of course, beautiful Queen Esther, were women of lovely appearance. It is also interesting to note that Esther spent twelve months making herself as beautiful as possible before going before the king. Esther 2:12 tells us she worked "six months with oil of myrrh, and six months with sweet odours, and with other things for the purifying of the women." God does not despise beauty; He loves it.

When Is Looking Attractive Wrong?

Looking attractive has often been associated with pride, vanity, and the seduction of men, thus ungodly, worldly, and sinful. The wrong is not in looking attractive but rather in *why* one is trying to look attractive. What is the motive? Is it to attract the attention of men in a seductive way? Is it to impress others with our image or money? How does looking attractive fit into our priorities? Are we spending more time on our personal appearance than on our spiritual growth? Are we better known for how we look than for what we are?

Jezebel adorned herself for evil reasons. She was a vicious, wicked person and her appearance reflected it. No amount of cosmetics or dress could cover up such evil motives and wickedness. On the other hand, Esther used her natural beauty and appearance, not for selfish reasons, but for the glory of God.

There is a definite contrast between an ungodly woman's use of appearance to seduce or do evil and the beauty and influence of a godly woman. When we use appearance for selfish, evil reasons, it is wrong! When we with moderation use our attractiveness for the Lord's glory, it is right and good.

Choosing Our Clothing

One may wonder why some women look all put together, just right, while others look all thrown together, all wrong. We perhaps go to our closets only to find "nothing" to wear, or to an occasion, maybe even church, and wish we could hide under the carpet. The secret to avoiding such feelings is knowing how to plan and choose your clothing.

This subject is too vast to cover in one chapter, but there are some principles that can be mentioned in hopes that interest will be created to inspire a personal study of this subject. Many books are available in the library and bookstores that give very helpful and detailed information.

The qualifications needed for looking our best are: interest, desire, effort, and honesty. Start with a full-length mirror. It is vital to focus on the person we are dressing—ourselves. Often we spend a lifetime buying and wearing clothes just because they look good on a model, in a picture, or on someone else. God made each of us to be different, however. We come in all colors, sizes, and shapes. It is logical then that we will not all look good in the same clothing.

The first step is to analyze ourselves. We begin with our posture because even the most exquisite dress looks sloppy on a drooping body. Next, being completely honest, we decide on our body type by asking ourselves questions like, "Am I tall, short, or average?" "Am I thin, average, or plump?" "Do I have a long neck, broad shoulders, small waist, heavy hips, or the opposites?" We honestly list our assets as well as our "imperfections."

The big secret to looking our best is to emphasize our assets and camouflage that which we do not want to draw attention to. For example, if someone has big hips, she can draw attention away from her hips by wearing light colors on top, broad-shoulder styles, and lots of emphasis such as yokes, puffy sleeves, and attention-getting scarves or collars in the neck and shoulder area. This draws the eye upward and away from the hips. Much information is available to help a lady in maximizing her assets. We can study, learn, and practice. It works!

Fashion comes and goes, but a person's style is good for all times. Style is an expression of a person's personality. Most of us have been shopping, seen a dress, and exclaimed, "This looks just like Susie." That is because Susie has learned to express her personality through a particular style. Some women seem to *fit* in ruffles and soft fabrics while others are perfect in the classic suit. "What style do I really feel like myself in?" we should ask. It is vital that a person's style fits her personality. We need to avoid fashion trends unless we can say, "That is my style. That is me!"

It is really true! Color is one of the best considerations for the wardrobe. Because God loves variety, He has made us in different colors—some blondes, some redheads, and some brunettes. And with each coloring He made the perfect tones of eyes and skin to go with it. We can enhance the perfect creation that God has made us by wearing clothes in colors that look best with our natural coloring.

Someone may ask a lady who is feeling great, "Are you feeling okay? You look pale today." Possibly the lady was wearing the wrong color of clothing. On the other hand, she could be feeling bad and wearing the "right" color and receive many compliments. Proper color selection is a big factor in looking radiant, alive, and lovely. Color is a very interesting study and many books are now available on this subject.

When one has honestly analyzed her body type, her personality style, and her coloring, she is ready to dress the real her. By this time she is beginning to realize that she has many "mistakes" in her closet—wrong style, wrong colors. Few ladies can afford a new wardrobe, but a person can begin with her next purchase. The next time she shops, she can ask herself these questions:

- Is it decent and modest?
- Is it a good color for me?
- Does it enhance my figure by maximizing my assets and camouflaging my "flaws"?
- Is it just a fashion trend or is it my style and will it last several seasons?
- Is it a good investment and is it within my budget?
- When I wear this, will it testify to the glory and beauty of my God?

The final step to consider is accessories. The right accessories can make an inexpensive dress look great while wrong ones can make an expensive dress look cheap. A big problem is impulse buying. Something that catches the eye or is on sale is a temptation, but will it go with anything in the closet? The secret is in one word, *blending*. Some women's accessories are like flashing lights—they are all one can see. Shoes, handbag, scarf, hat, belt, and hose should blend, not distract, creating a head-to-toe total image.

Because we do not indulge in jewelry, makeup, and other such "additions," sometimes we have a tendency to overdo what we do wear. Simplicity is elegant while too much of anything is in bad taste.

Add all of this to a healthy, clean body. Top it off with a neat, attractive hairstyle—again, not overdone. Add a touch of mild, lovely perfume and a radiant, sincere smile and you will feel great because you will look great!

Minding Your Manners

How many times have we heard the expression, "Pretty is as pretty does"? It is not enough to look good, we must act good. How we express ourselves in word and action has a definite effect on the total image of how we look.

Manners can be defined as a way of addressing and treating others. Everyone has manners. Some have good manners, others bad manners. Many books have been written on etiquette, which is basically codes of conduct that are accepted by our culture as a proper way to act and dress in various social situations.

Often these rules are updated due to a changing world and lifestyles. However, manners are never out-of-date because it is never wrong to be temperate, modest, kind, and considerate. Manners are outward manifestations of how we feel and are inside. They reveal our character, our morals, and how we feel about other people. If we truly love others as we are commanded to, we will not want to offend them in any way. This is the basis of good manners.

It dishonors God when a Christian is rude, thoughtless, inconsiderate, disruptive, "pushy," or verbally or physically offensive. Our Christian witness is never more on display than when we are in unpleasant or stressful social situations. Solomon admonished us, Greater is "he that ruleth his spirit than he that taketh a city" (Proverbs 16:32).

Good manners can be summed up in two verses of Scripture. Jesus said, "Love the Lord thy God with all thy heart . . . love thy neighbour as thyself" (Mark 12:30-31). "All things whatsoever ye would that men should do to you, do ye even so to them" (Matthew 7:12). These verses of Scripture can be applied in every situation and under any circumstances. Living by these principles automatically produces good manners.

The Final Touches

Today's woman lives in a world where femininity is being attacked through an effort to drastically change the image, values, roles, and actions of women. A cartoon pictured a minister marrying a shaggy, unisex-clad couple. He ended by saying, "Now will one of you please kiss the bride."

Christian women must strive to accentuate the differences between themselves and the masculine male. God chose to make a distinct difference between male and female. This distinction is vividly propagated throughout the Bible and should be exemplified in the gentle, soft, feminine qualities found in a Christian woman's appearance, manner, and actions.

A gentle, quiet spirit is better adornment than the most elaborate attire. The Bible indicates that Queen Esther's natural care and beauty was enough for she required nothing but what was appointed (Esther 2:15). A Christian woman does not need worldly ornamentation for "He will beautify the meek with salvation" and "The king's daughter is all glorious within." (See Psalm 149:4; 45:13.) God does not condemn beauty in women. He does make it clear that we are not to depend upon outward appearance, but rather upon inner beauty which comes from our relationship with God.

It is never too late to learn or improve. As a lady improves her appearance, she will gain a sense of satisfaction because she will have enhanced her Christian witness and accomplished something of lasting value. Her life will be richer and more satisfying. A wise woman steps through doors of improvement and avails herself of opportunities to learn and grow. She becomes a challenge to herself and an inspiration to others.

"Let your light so shine before men, that they may see your good works, and glorify your Father which is in heaven" (Matthew 5:16). That gives real meaning and purpose to looking great—to putting one's best face forward.

Test Your Knowledge

True or False

_____ 1. Our appearance has nothing to do with our Christian testimony to others.

_____ 2. The Bible speaks of the beauty of women in a positive, not negative, way.

_____ 3. Looking attractive is wrong only when the motive is wrong, when it is used for selfish or evil purposes.

_____ 4. Everyone can look great in any style or color.

_____ 5. A secret to looking our best is to emphasize our assets and "camouflage" that to which we do not wish to call attention.

_____ 6. Accessories should blend, not distract, helping to create a total, head-to-toe image.

_____ 7. In our modern, anything-goes society, Christians need no longer consider good manners so important.

_____ 8. Femininity has nothing to do with Christianity.

_____ 9. A quiet, gentle spirit is better adornment than the most elaborate attire.

Apply Your Knowledge

Look back over the chapter and carry out the suggestions made for planning and choosing your clothing. Go through your wardrobe to make sure everything is in good repair, clean, and pressed. It may also be possible to improve or update some of your clothing with alterations or by adding a scarf or blouse in a better color for you. Spend some extra time in God's Word and in prayer in order to improve your inner beauty.

Expand Your Knowledge

Do a study on the women of the Bible to obtain a better understanding of the kind of woman God wants us to be. Obtain books from the library or bookstore on clothing, style, color, and etiquette to improve your knowledge in these areas.

10. Your Crowning Glory

But if a woman have long hair, it is a glory to her: for her hair is given her for a covering.
I Corinthians 11:15

> **Start with the Scriptures**
> Psalm 119:89, 105
> Proverbs 22:6
> I Corinthians 11:1-16; 14:37
> I Timothy 2:9
> James 1:21-22
> I Peter 3:3-4

"How long is long?" one person may ask. Another question, "Is it okay to cut my hair as long as it is still long?" Still others might make statements such as, "Short hair is prettier than long hair," or "If I trim the ends, my hair will grow better and be more healthy."

Such are familiar statements made by some women who simply do not understand the principles established in God's Word concerning hair on ladies or else they choose not to obey the Scriptures and they desire to justify their actions. But as Christians we cannot afford to ignore scriptural principles, nor can we treat them casually for the sake of convenience. The Scriptures clearly establish the necessity of and purpose for women having long, uncut hair, and we are wise to open our heart and rightly divide or correctly analyze God's Word. (See II Timothy 2:15.)

The Authority of the Scriptures

The apostle Paul, the writer of the Book of I Corinthians, dealt specifically with the subject of a woman's glory—her hair. His authority as an apostle and the divine inspiration of the epistles he wrote are without question. Yet even in his day he faced critics who would attempt to deny his authority. He nonetheless stood firm and wrote with authority to the churches and Christians of that time and, ultimately, to all Christians.

Paul wrote twice in the first Corinthian epistle that they should follow him as he followed Christ (I Corinthians 4:16; 11:1). The word *follow* is translated from the Greek word *mimitais*, which literally means to "imitate." Paul further qualified his writings as the commandments of God: "If any man think himself to be a prophet, or spiritual, let him acknowledge that the things that I write unto you are the commandments of the Lord" (I Corinthians 14:37).

God's Word is forever established and settled in heaven (Psalm 119:89). We as Christians are to receive and welcome it as it is the only source for salvation. Only as we obey the Bible can we know salvation in Jesus Christ. "Wherefore lay apart all filthiness and superfluity of naughtiness, and receive with meekness the engrafted word, which is able to save your souls. But be ye doers of the word, and not hearers only, deceiving your own selves" (James 1:21-22).

The Bible which has come to us by means of the miraculous, preserving power of God, is for our good. It is to our benefit to submit to the teachings of the Word of God and apply them to our lives.

As we study the Scriptures, especially as they pertain to women's hair, we should realize that it is God's Word and His will for us. As such, it is for our benefit; He has our best interests in mind.

Not only are our interests at stake in our response as ladies to God's Word, but also those of our children, especially girls. We are to teach our children and be examples for them to follow.

The Word of God exhorts us to "Train up a child in the way he should go: and when he is old, he will not depart from it" (Proverbs 22:6). According to *Webster's Ninth New Collegiate Dictionary*, *train* means "to form by instruction, discipline, or drill; to teach so as to make fit, qualified, or proficient; to make prepared for a test of skill; to aim at an object or objective." All of our discipline, nurture, instruction, and warnings must be framed with one ultimate objective in mind: to bring our children to a point where they become obedient disciples of Jesus Christ.

Today we might have a little, innocent girl. The training and discipline that we give her now will determine what kind of woman she will become tomorrow. That training is done not only in word, but also in example—that which we ourselves do.

Some Basic Definitions

"Every man praying or prophesying, having his head covered, dishonoureth his head. But every woman that prayeth or prophesieth with her head uncovered dishonoureth her head: for that is even all one as if she were shaven. For if the woman be not covered, let her also be shorn: but if it be a shame for a woman to be shorn or shaven, let her be covered" (I Corinthians 11:4-6).

The following definitions are offered from *Webster's Ninth New Collegiate Dictionary.*

Shave—"to remove a thin layer from, to cut off in thin layers or shreds, to cut off closely; to sever the hair . . . close to the roots."

Shorn—(past participle of *shear*, so we must define the word *shear*.) "To cut off the hair from, to cut or clip (as hair or wool) from someone or something, to cut or trim with shears or a similar instrument; to cut with something sharp."

It is interesting to note that the dictionary defines *shear* as simply meaning "to cut," without specifying how much. In other words, to trim is to cut or shear whether the removed amount of hair is little or much. The action is technically the same.

The Principle of Submission

We can only fully understand I Corinthians 11:1-16 when we recognize the basic premise upon which it was written. The subject of hair on men and women is not the primary one of this passage of Scripture. Rather, the primary subject is that of relationships and submission to authority. "But I would have you know, that the head of every man is Christ; and the head of the woman is the man; and the head of Christ is God" (I Corinthians 11:3). This principle of authority lies at the heart of the teaching on hair.

Paul wrote regarding the subject of hair consequentially as it related to the primary subject—submission to authority. This is not to say that because hair was not the primary concern of Paul it was unimportant. To the contrary, he wrote regarding it because of its importance in symbolizing complete submission to our scriptural heads of authority. The scriptural principle is that of submission to authority; the scriptural symbol of that submission is in the length of our hair.

An astute observation is made in the book, *Why? A Study of Christian Standards*, published by Word Aflame Publications. On page 46 the author writes, "It would be a mistake for either a man or a woman to adhere to a symbol [in this case long hair on women] while not fulfilling that which is symbolized [submission to authority]. But it would be equally erroneous for a person to assume that he could fulfill the reality of submission without the symbol which God has chosen to represent it."

A woman's appearance should be feminine and should reveal her submission to authority. Long hair on ladies has long been associated with femininity in practically every culture of the world. In recent years, however, in conjunction with the modern so-called feminist movement, that standard has been challenged. But it is not only a cultural distinction of the female; it is a scriptural mandate. She should not pray or prophesy "with her head uncovered" for to do so dishonors her head, the man, and ultimately Christ. (See I Corinthians 11:3-6.) "For the man is not of the woman; but the woman of the man. Neither was the man created for the woman; but the woman for the man" (I Corinthians 11:8-9).

The question then follows, "What is the covering which a woman should have?"

The Covering of the Woman

"Judge in yourselves: is it comely that a woman pray unto God uncovered? Doth not even nature itself teach you, that, if a man have long hair, it is a shame unto him? But if a woman have long hair, it is a glory to her: for her hair is given her for a covering" (I Corinthians 11:13-15).

The word *covered* (verse 6) as translated from the Greek means "covered fully" or "covered thoroughly." The word *covering* (verse 15) means "covered completely" or "covered all the way around." The word *covered* (verse 6) is a verb. It refers only to a condition—that of being covered. The word *covering* (verse 15), on the other hand, is a noun. It signifies the thing that is to "cover" the woman's head.

Until verse fifteen no item is fully identified as the article of covering, although Paul does use the words *shorn* and *shaven* in reference to hair and refers to hair in other verses such as verse ten and verse fourteen. In verse fifteen, however, Paul clearly identifies the noun, the article which does the act of covering, as hair—and not only hair, but he specifies "long hair."

Greek scholars Henry Thaer and W. E. Vine both define the Greek word *komao*, which is translated "long hair," as to "let the hair grow, to have long hair." The word signifies a present continuous process of allowing the hair to grow.

Long hair is hair that is allowed to grow. This idea contrasts sharply with the meaning of *shorn*, which is to cut with a sharp instrument. Hair cannot be allowed to grow and be cut at the same time. Long hair is not a specific length of hair. Rather it is hair that is allowed to grow uncut.

"Plainly, the words *shorn* and *long* are used as opposites. Since *keiro* [shorn] means to 'have one's hair cut' and *kome* [long hair] means 'uncut hair,' there is no doubt that a Christian woman should not cut her hair. If she cuts her hair, regardless of the amount, her hair has been shorn" (*Why, A Study of Christian Standards*, p. 48). And if it is a shame for a woman to be shorn or shaven, she should be covered (verses 5-6). The only scriptural covering is her long, uncut hair (verse 15).

To know to do good but to refuse to do it is a sin—the sin of rebellion. (See James 4:17.) Rebellion was the sin of Lucifer and the fallen angels. Possibly to emphasize the danger of rebellion, Paul referred to the angels as a reason to have "power" or "authority" (in the form of long hair) on the woman's head (verse 10). Since long hair on a woman's head is her covering and since it is a symbol of her submission to man and ultimately to God, she should follow the angels' example of obedience and reverence to God. Conversely, she should avoid Lucifer's and his angels' example of rebellion against God's plan.

Why Destroy the Glory?

The first sin to ever stain the purity of the universe was the sin of rebellion. Lucifer, through the pride of his heart, rebelled against the authority of God and refused to occupy the position that God had assigned him. He did not want God's authority over him. He was unwilling to submit to authority.

Some women cut their hair because of rebellion. Self-will is the cause of rebellion. For a woman to selfishly persist in her own will in opposition to the will of God, however, is open defiance against God's authority and the place He has assigned her. "For rebellion is as the sin of witchcraft, and stubbornness is as iniquity and idolatry" (I Samuel 15:23).

Some women cut their hair because they have never come into the knowledge of God's truth in this matter. The thing that is important is not what a person has done in the past, for God forgives sin. What is important is what we do with our life today and in the future. Past sins are put under Christ's shed blood, and we can set our affections on the Lord Jesus Christ to serve Him fully with all our heart. "Judgment must begin at the house of God" (I Peter 4:17).

Some women have never cut their hair but have not established a personal conviction on the subject. This is a dangerous position. They are open to the deceitfulness of Satan. If they do not know and understand the Word of God, when Satan casts doubt on its validity, they listen. But if we know the truth it will "set us free." "My people are destroyed for lack of knowledge" (Hosea 4:6).

Knowing and understanding what God expects of us will prevent us from being ashamed of our long hair. Our desire is to please God more than man. But to know and understand God's Word requires dedicated study of its precious truths (II Timothy 2:15).

"And wisdom and knowledge shall be the stability of thy times, and strength of salvation: the fear of the LORD is his treasure" (Isaiah 33:6). Making a study of God's plan for hair on women will give us stability and strength. Then our hair will become the glory (dignity, honor, praise, worship) to us that it was intended to be. Rather than regarding our hair as a "mop" or as "trouble," it will remind us of our honorable place before God and man.

No Other Custom

As Paul concluded his discourse of the first part of I Corinthians 11, he made an interesting statement that has been much food for thought and, unfortunately at times, misunderstanding. "But if any man seem to be contentious, we have no such custom, neither the churches of God" (I Corinthians 11:16). The *Amplified Bible* offers an insightful translation of this verse: "Now if any one is disposed to be argumentative and contentious about this, we hold to and recognize no other custom [in worship] than this, nor do the churches of God generally."

It is ludicrous to think that the apostle Paul would take fifteen verses of Scripture to discuss the principle of submission to authority and the symbol of that submission, hair, and then destroy his teaching with one verse. Paul was *not* saying, "We won't be contentious about this subject because it really doesn't matter anyway." Rather Paul was underscoring the importance of that which he had taught. Simply, he was affirming that there was no other custom in the church than that of a woman being covered while praying or prophesying. And he had already clearly stated what that covering is—long hair.

Seven Reasons To Have Uncut Hair

In their book, *In Search of Holiness*, authors David and Loretta Bernard give seven reasons why a woman should have uncut hair.

1. Uncut hair is a sign of her submission to authority.
2. The angels are watching to see if she has this "mark."
3. It is a shame for a woman to pray or prophesy with an uncovered head. Hair is her covering, and if she cuts her hair it is the same as being completely shaven.
4. Nature teaches her to have long hair as opposed to shorn hair (cut hair) or a shaven head.
5. Long hair is her glory.
6. She is a type of the church and her uncut hair is a type (sign) of the church's submission to Christ.
7. It is one of God's methods for maintaining a distinction between male and female.

Modest Hairstyles

The only commandments of God concerning a woman fixing her hair pertains to modesty. "Also [I desire] that women should adorn themselves modestly and appropriately and sensibly in seemly apparel, not with [elaborate] hair arrangement or gold or pearls or expensive clothing" (I Timothy 2:9, *Amplified Bible*).

"Let not yours be the [merely] external adorning with [elaborate] interweaving and knotting of the hair, the wearing of jewelry, or changes of clothes; But let it be the inward adorning and beauty of the hidden person of the heart, with the incorruptible and unfading charm of a gentle and peaceful spirit, which (is not anxious or wrought up, but) is very precious in the sight of God" (I Peter 3:3-4, *Amplified Bible*).

Hair should not be fixed in elaborate hairstyles as to draw attention to oneself. It should be modest and moderate. A woman should radiate the beauty of the Lord and the grace of a godly lady.

Pentecostal ladies are known by the world for their long hair. They should be neat and well-kept in order to glorify Jesus Christ. We are representatives of the living God on assignment to win the lost. People should see Christ reflected in us.

The philosophy of the world is that one must look young to be beautiful. Some women will do practically anything within their power to remain young looking. Perhaps this is why dyes and tints have become a fad in the world, but even hairdressers agree that dyes and tints are very hard on a person's hair. God color-coordinated our complexion, our eyes, and our hair. Our tampering with His color scheme is not His plan for our lives and is actually an insult to God.

"The hoary [gray or white with age] head is a crown of glory, if it be found in the way of righteousness" (Proverbs 16:31).

The Lord simply wants Christian ladies to be modest in every way. As our moderation is known to others we bring a special glory to God. We learn how to contentedly accept ourselves as God made us, but also how to present ourselves in modesty and godliness both inwardly (spirit) and outwardly (flesh). (See II Corinthians 7:1.)

As we accept our place in God and His kingdom, we will learn to cherish the glory that He has given especially to us—long, beautiful hair. A Christian radiance will shine forth from our lives and attract others to the Lord Jesus Christ. Not only will our hair be a crowning glory, but our entire person will be a true glory to Christ.

God, who knows all things and does all things well, has established an order of authority and headship in our world. As a lady understands and submits to this order, she comes under the umbrella of its blessings and protection. Submission will enable her to fully appreciate her "crowning glory."

Test Your Knowledge

1. Describe the order of authority given in I Corinthians 11:3.
2. Define the words *shorn* and *shaven* as used in I Corinthians 11.
3. "Long hair" is hair that is allowed to _____.
4. A woman's long hair is her _____.
5. Define the words "hoary head."
6. What are the seven reasons why a woman should have uncut hair?

Apply Your Knowledge

After studying this subject thoroughly, a woman should purpose in her heart to continually leave her hair uncut and to wear it in a neat and modest fashion. A firm conviction of this truth and an appreciation for God's plan and protection of authority will enable each lady to portray a grateful attitude toward her "crowning glory."

Expand Your Knowledge

Because of limited space this chapter has only been a brief examination of the subject of women's hair. Possibly you will want to study the subject further.

There are several excellent books that deal with the subject of hair. You may wish to continue your study through the use of the following books.

- *Why? A Study of Christian Standards* by Word Aflame Publications.
- *Hair Length in the Bible* by Daniel Segraves, Word Aflame Press.
- *In Search of Holiness* by David and Loretta Bernard, Word Aflame Press.
- *Covered by Love* by Ladies Ministries.

These books are available through the Pentecostal Publishing House, 8855 Dunn Road, Hazelwood, MO 63042-2299 (*www.pentecostalpublishing.com* and 866-819-7667).

11. Teaching Principles and Standards

Train up a child in the way he should go: and when he is old, he will not depart from it.
Proverbs 22:6

Start with the Scriptures
Deuteronomy 6:7
Psalm 119:9
Romans 8:1-2; 12:1, 21
I Corinthians 3:16-17; 6:12; 15:33
II Corinthians 6:17; 7:1
I Thessalonians 5:22
II Timothy 2:1-5, 11-13
Titus 2:3-4

"Who has the right to tell me what to do?" is the hot question of today. The important thing to remember is that no one can live without authority. Sure, there are a few who have radical standards, just as there are some policemen who are not perfect, but we would not want to live without policemen.

Youth who rebel at the authority of their parents will find another form of authority such as opinions of teachers, peers, or the prevalent standard of the world. A question arises and its answer will come from some predominant standard. Christian sources for authority on standards must be biblically derived.

Contrasts Within the Church

People today are morally confused. Standards and values of dress, attitudes, and manners are crumbling. The world is on fast-running rapids of carelessness, crudeness, and vague generalities. To a degree this has entered into the church through the atmosphere of the world and the slackness of teaching. Sin has clouded many minds.

The number of aborted babies thrown into oblivion expresses the lack of value placed on human life. There is a discarding of permanent marriage in the world, and even in some churches. Some are divorced and remarried in the same church while some ministers are not even sure of what they believe about this. This causes perplexity among youth.

Inadequate Christian education causes distress and the inability to think clearly. Bad judgment results, and people revert to their own reasoning, ignoring the Word of God. There is a battle for the mind.

In the September 1987 issue of *Good Housekeeping*, an article entitled "The Alcohol Epidemic" states that twenty-three percent of thirteen-year-old girls and thirty percent of thirteen-year-old boys drink regularly. Two basic causes of this are television and uncaring parents. Yet many unthinking Christians have televisions in their homes, by which children are taught that adultery, drinking, immodest dress, and homosexuality are acceptable lifestyles.

Some so-called Christian music is questionable, as is the term "Christian rock." All popular music is not morally wrong, but some of the pulsation that comes from the guitars and percussion instruments certainly evoke a sensuous response from the human body. Christian music must center on words that carry a message and not rely upon physiological responses.

Several years ago people were leaving traditional churches because they were spiritually dead. Today there are churches with religious emotion but without morals! Emphasis is sometimes on revival with no time for practical teaching. The youth, therefore, go without learning basic standards, violating the inner teaching of the Holy Ghost, while they keep the standards of the non-church world. This creates guilt and restlessness.

Contrasts with the World

There is a contrast between the world and church regarding things such as sports, body movements, speech, clothing, showing of affections, and attitudes. For example, in spectator sports the attitude is to win regardless of the cost. The atmosphere that surrounds such sporting events involves cursing, immodest clothing, drinking, and a general riotous spirit.

Worldly, sensual body movements, speech, and attitudes which are seen and heard daily can be absorbed into the lifestyle of Christian youth if they are not aware of the battle to be fought. They need to know how to react and know the principles of holiness so that they will be equipped to make their own moral decisions.

Youth need to have guidelines for single dating. Every date should have planned activities and a set time schedule. When teenagers go shopping, dating, or visiting, there is a need to give them a time to return home. Parental guidance and consistent guidelines will help our youth to "flee youthful lusts." The ideal situation is for parents to be parenting, and the church to be reinforcing parental guidelines.

Another problem trend is in the area of jewelry. Unadorned watches are useful, but moderation should be our guiding principles. As the world trend escalates toward more and more jewelry with sometimes multiple rings for each finger, Christian young people absorb this if not checked. This is worldliness. These things cause problems among the youth because they see inconsistency and no principle upon which to build their lives. Caution and modesty are absolutely essential.

Contradictions in the Church

Contradictions in the church create problems. For instance, some people might use artificially colored wigs for convenience, while the youth are taught not to color their cheeks or dye their hair. Parents who cannot control their temper when the people in the next car honk their horn, contradict any teaching the young people receive from Bible lessons on the fruit of the Spirit.

Theaters are banned, but some parents rent worldly motion picture videos for their children to view while they are busy. This inconsistency perplexes youth. The abusive, vulgar language, love triangles, and ungodly dress in such movies create a double standard.

Purpose of Teaching Standards and Values

Standards are used as a base for measuring and judging value and quality. God has given man a conscience to govern actions, but it is only dependable when the correct information has been programmed into it. We must teach God's Word, for it is the authentic authority. Holiness cannot be legislated; however, teaching biblical standards helps people willingly to separate themselves to God and from the world.

The ABC's of Divine Standards

The reason for teaching principles and standards from the Word is to awaken the fear of God that might prompt obedience. The fear of God is the substance of sanity and common sense, that is, the "beginning of knowledge" (Proverbs 1:7).

Age and experience have not yet given youth the ability to assess many things. They cannot think things out with human reasoning. Many times things that seem logical to them are shortsighted and against biblical principles. Someone needs to help young people and ground them in the Word of God.

Classification of Standards

There are several classifications of standards which must be taught. They are: ❶ standards taught by explicit verses of Scripture that designate a subject as sin; ❷ standards derived from biblical principles of holiness; ❸ standards formulated by a body of God-ordained ministers; and ❹ standards resulting from social values and customs.

Some verses of Scripture clearly designate a subject as sin, such as do not commit murder and do not lie.

Verses of Scripture that teach "Love not the world," and "Your body is the temple of the Holy Ghost" give standards that are derived from biblical principles of holiness. Loving the world means that a person is more conscious of himself and the world than he is of God. Knowledge of this fact reveals that some things of the world are evil even though the Scriptures do not explicitly name them. By our bodies being designated as the temples of the Holy Ghost, we know that even if there were no verses of Scripture against alcoholic drinks, it is still in principle unacceptable. This principle includes smoking and taking drugs which are not explicitly named in the Scriptures as sin.

Standards also are derived from the collective wisdom of a body of ministers. Ministers can determine whether something should be avoided because it is unbecoming to saints, borders on sin, or its indulgence can lead away from God. The minister is within bounds to set standards because he is commissioned to watch for and give an account of the souls which are in his care (Hebrews 13:17). For this reason, ministers do meet, discuss current issues from a biblical viewpoint, and decide some standards. The apostolic church practiced this (Acts 15:1-29).

Social values and customs also dictate some standards. Custom is conformity to social rules and usually becomes a guide of life. The secular world widely uses guidelines and standards. Dress codes are posted for the medical profession, universities, factories and even some restaurants. Guidelines are given so that people will know what standards are expected. Since they have an interest in or are privileged to be associated with the company or school, they obey. There is no conflict, no guessing and no errors.

Some standards in the church are derived from social mores and customs. Some attire, which may not be scripturally immodest, may not be the proper attire to wear to a funeral, certain restaurants, or to church. Ministers of the gospel are required by custom and social rules to wear certain types of attire. If Christians ignore dress values of custom and society, they will not be able to effectively carry out the commission God has given them. Of course, the Word of God is the ultimate authority, so when biblical principles and customs conflict, we abide by God's Word.

Biblical teachings must be communicated with consistency. Since there are clear, fair, Bible standards and principles, there is a target for which to aim. By explaining in language and illustrations on the student's level, he can then understand and identify with the teaching.

Be Aware and Be Ready to Answer

Youth must learn to assess the value of their salvation, their name, their chastity, and their honor. When temptations come, the learned value system takes control and a quick, correct decision can be made! They must learn to make decisions based upon their convictions of what the Scriptures teach.

One of the most successful ways of avoiding a distressful situation is to know, in advance, what to say when approached. For instance, if someone says, "Let's buy a beer" or someone makes sexual advances, the youth should be so thoroughly taught until he would react boldly, "I do not do that."

Essentiality of Positive Teaching

The fate of the church hinges upon strong, clear teaching of biblical standards to youth. If they are not biblically educated on how Christians are to dress and behave, they will be lost, endangering the future of the church. The kind of teaching that leads to a happy, productive and successful Christian life is *positive* teaching.

Happiness is not a matter of good fortune or material possessions. It comes from a right mental attitude toward God. Christians are not "legalists under bondage." God wants them to have an appreciation for His standards of holiness. He does not want them to be miserable over the negative things they do not do!

God's Law

The definition of *law* includes "power to enforce, advise, and exhort." A driver is warned not to enter a freeway exit by a sign that states "DO NOT ENTER." The power of enforcement is implied, but this is not negative. Laws are good and positive.

Children and youth should strive to know God's laws concerning standards and realize they are meant to keep them from danger of eternal death!

The Instructor's Qualifications

A person has a one-time privilege to enter heaven. There is no second chance. It is vital that the youth be taught by qualified instructors. Eternal life is at stake.

Essentiality of Teaching Youth

Learning is more than mere knowledge. If a person memorizes all the Scriptures and chooses to act differently, he has not learned. Learning involves experiences and corrections along the way so that knowledge acquired is practiced in everyday life.

Discipline, the First Step

It is urgent that we begin with discipline because "train up a child" means to guide, to discipline, to condition, and make fit. The Bible does not teach us to force the child, but to discipline, guide and train him, until his training is an understood and practiced lifestyle. We should not construe this to mean children should not be pressed to attend church, but rather, parents and teachers should be certain children understand the essentiality of church attendance. Teaching is not a matter of pouring information into empty minds, but it is helping youth to understand and apply what is learned into everyday changes and improvements.

The Home, the Primary Source of Learning

The humanistic invasion of the home tries to make each family and individual a deity, full of greed and selfishness. This ideology has entered some church members and produced some parents who simply do not have time for their children.

The church is sometimes expected to do all the teaching of biblical principles and is blamed if this is not accomplished. In like manner, public schools are expected to do all the teaching of secular knowledge and social graces. However, learning is an every-moment situation where, rightly or wrongly, children are taught basic discipline, manners, and moral standards. This occurs primarily at home.

If the home does not shoulder this responsibility properly, then the church does not have a foundation upon which to teach biblical principles and standards. For example, if a child lies and it is not detected because of a minimum of family time, how can morals be effectively taught from the church?

Parents, then, must be the primary teachers. They are the only authoritative figures a child knows in his formative years. Mothers who work outside the home are leaving their children with people who will be an essential part of the child's learning process. The life of these caretakers either underscores or contradicts what the child is taught at home and church. If there is a contradiction, the child will be confused.

Parents need to make a commitment that their child will be as informed about the Bible as they are their "three R's." Parents need to teach and leave nothing for the church to do except re-emphasize what has already been taught! Parents should construct stories of everyday life with morals for their young children. For example, the time to teach teenagers about the kind of person they should marry is before they are teenagers! They need to understand that only people of like faith should marry.

Children and teenagers should be taught that people have different values and lifestyles. Those who attend the same church but have different standards and principles do not make good dating choices. Even Paul taught there were some in the church with whom you should not have fellowship (II Thessalonians 3:6, 11, 14).

Inner Church Problems

In the church sometimes pastors and parents force young people to do that which is right, without giving thought as to whether they understand or obey from their heart. In this atmosphere, hypocrites are sometimes born, nurtured, and thrive. Rebellion could be a sign that the young person is really asking for help, or saying, "Understand me and explain why."

Focus needs to be on the Scriptures and biblical principles so that decisions can be made from the heart, and not from memorized rules. When emphasis is on principles and they are understood, they will be obeyed. Commitment to God is needed instead of only emotional church experiences and inadequately understood principles of holiness. Let us teach youth to be true to themselves, their parents, and most of all to God.

Test Your Knowledge

1. Name the four classifications of standards.
2. There are contrasts with the world and church, but are there ever contradictions in the church? Explain your answer.
3. According to the lesson, who has the right to tell us what to do?
4. Why should parents and teachers be knowledgeable and have a special interest in biblical teaching?

Apply Your Knowledge

When the church fails the youth by not teaching biblical standards, their chances of entering heaven are limited. Learning is not merely accumulating facts, but is the ability to apply knowledge, obeying and making corrections in life to be ready for heaven. The ultimate responsibility for youth falls upon their parents. If parents fail, the church must take up the slack, even though the church only has them for a minimum of time. Souls are at stake!

Expand Your Knowledge

As a helper to the pulpit ministry, you have positions as parents and teachers to teach the Word. Use the passages of Scripture found in this chapter that teach principles and make a list of things you feel are worldly, bordering on sin, or are actually sinful. If you make personal conclusions and obtain personal convictions, your teaching will be dynamic.

A great book from Ladies Ministries is *The Girl in the Dress* by Lori Wagner. Written especially for girls, this is an excellent study book for uncovering the mystery of modesty. Also consider the following books: *Modesty* by Nan Pamer, *Why? A Study of Christian Standards* by Word Aflame Publications, and *Practical Holiness: A Second Look* by David K. Bernard.

These books are available through the Pentecostal Publishing House, 8855 Dunn Road, Hazelwood, MO 63042-2299 (*www.pentecostalpublishing.com* and 866-819-7667).

Come to My House

12

Be not forgetful to entertain strangers: for thereby some have entertained angels unawares.
Hebrews 13:2

Start with the Scriptures
Genesis 18:1-5
II Kings 4:8-21
Acts 2:46; 16:15, 33-34; 18:1-3, 24-27; 20:9-12, 20
I Corinthians 16:15-19
I Timothy 3:2; 5:9-10
Titus 1:8

The home has always been an important place to entertain and fellowship. Christian ladies are often called upon to be hospitable. Some are just born to be gracious hostesses, but most of us have to learn the graces of hospitality. Many ladies panic at the chime of their front doorbell and yet we can learn to enjoy opening our homes to guests. It has been said that a gracious hostess takes care of all her guest's needs better than the guest could for himself.

The Bible is full of accounts of gracious hosts and hostesses. In each account we find the hosts going out of their way to provide for the needs of their guest. Sometimes it was a good friend, a weary stranger, or even angels!

Entertaining Angels Unaware

Abraham, who was called the friend of God, and Sarah, his wife, knew how to offer hospitality. In Genesis 18:1-5 Abraham honored three strange men as they approached his tent by bowing toward the ground. He then invited them to rest themselves under his trees while he obtained water and food for them. He hastened into the tent, where Sarah was, and asked her to quickly make cakes while he ran to the field to slay a tender young calf to roast for them. He provided the best of everything he had for his guests.

After these guests had eaten and been refreshed, it was then that they shared the good news from God that Abraham and Sarah (who were well past the age of bearing children) would certainly bear a son. They also shared with Abraham the knowledge that Sodom and Gommorah would soon be destroyed. What Abraham would have missed had he not taken time to entertain these strangers! At least two of these strangers were angels and one of them seems to have been a manifestation of God, yet it appears that Abraham entertained his guests very cordially even before realizing their divine and heavenly natures.

Entertaining Is A Soulwinning Tool

The early church grew as they went from house to house visiting and talking of the good things of God. Acts 2:46 tells us, "And they, continuing daily with one accord in the temple, and breaking bread from house to house, did eat their meat with gladness and singleness of heart." The next verse tells us that they found favor with all people and the Lord added daily to the church.

Fellowship outside the church in a home setting is definitely beneficial to soulwinning. Too many times we find ourselves inviting the same comfortable friends over and fail to utilize one of the greatest tools of evangelism we have. Our home, be it ever so humble, along with a cup of hot cocoa or steamy cup of coffee can warm the heart of the unsaved and open the door of conversation to the beautiful truths of God's Word.

Many times sinners have looked at the church and felt like Christians were a strange sect of people. However, their perspective changed completely when they discovered the Christian enjoys eating, laughing, and having a good, clean time together. The sinner's wall of resistance crumbles when he feels on common ground with the Christian. A church atmosphere sometimes makes the sinner feel very uncomfortable, whereas a home setting provides a less threatening approach.

Jesus realized the importance of home ministry. He had no home to entertain guests in but He made arrangements to visit with Zacchaeus in a home environment when He sensed his hunger for truth (Luke 19:1-10).

Dinner Engagements

The first rule of entertaining successfully is to be relaxed or at least make an honest effort to appear that way. Running around in a dither or complaining about how hard we have worked only makes our guests uncomfortable and sense that they are a real bother.

When we stop and think of favorite times spent in someone's home, we will remember the kind of atmosphere they created that made us feel welcome. Normally what makes us feel most comfortable in someone else's home is what will make our guests feel welcome in our home. We can make it a habit to verbally tell our guests that we are glad they are visiting us and then let our actions express the same.

One should organize herself so that she will have everything ready for her guests long before their arrival time. She also needs to allow time for those inevitable emergencies that always seem to come up when preparing for company. By having the home clean, the table set and the food prepared, she will have a few minutes to attend to her personal grooming before the doorbell is due to ring. This will give her more confidence and allow her to be more relaxed to entertain her guests.

A lady should never make excuses for anything! If she does not have the finest china, or her roast burned a little around the edges, she ignores the fact and puts her guests at ease by being at ease! By her becoming genuinely interested in something that they feel comfortable discussing, they will enjoy her hospitality.

It may be more fun to talk about *our* kid's antics, *our* operation, or our vacation, but we must let them talk about theirs. They will enjoy themselves immensely, and that really is our goal. We should not discuss anything that would cause any of our guests to feel uncomfortable or that we would mind anyone else hearing. Pleasant, positive conversation always lifts the spirit. Negative conversation, even if we mean well, can cause disharmony as well as indigestion!

One should try to find out if there is any dietary restrictions her guests have before she plans her menu. Taking that into consideration, her meal will be enjoyed by all who are present at her table. It is a good idea to make note of a particular dish the guest really enjoyed. She can prepare it especially for the next time that person is in her home, and the guest will feel special, knowing that she remembered.

Usually it is best to prepare familiar recipes for our guests. Experiments with new recipes have often spelled disaster! If we are not sure of our guests' likes and dislikes, we need to have enough variety that they can choose something they will enjoy.

We should never insist that a guest eat something they hesitate about eating, nor should we insist they eat more than they want. There are many reasons why a guest will refuse a certain dish or a second helping, and it causes them embarrassment if you insist.

We should have our table set with the best that we have. A clean, ironed tablecloth or fresh place mats make any table setting special. A small centerpiece that does not obstruct the view of our guests is always pleasant, whether it is fresh flowers from the yard or a special arrangement from the florist.

A lady can consult a book from the local library on different table settings. If she is serving an ethnic meal, her decoration could reflect something from that country or culture. A seafood dinner could be complemented with something that reminds the guests of the sea, and an old-fashioned dinner could have something that reminds the guests of Grandma's house. These little touches add a little special atmosphere to her home and let her guests know she thinks they are special enough to do a little extra for them.

We should consider the social status of our guests and be sure that we do not make things so fancy that they would feel uncomfortable. Being sensitive to our guest's needs will cause our home to be a favorite place for them to come.

Overnight Guests

There will be times when we need to entertain guests overnight. Whether the guest room is a spare bedroom or our child's room, we need to spend a night in it. It is the only way to make sure there are no hidden discomforts. An ideal guest room is private and has its own or a nearby bathroom. The sheets should, of course, be freshly changed, and it is a good idea to keep an extra set of linens along with an extra pillow in the closet. The extra pillow should be a different size from those on the guest bed. This will give the guest a choice and hopefully a more restful night.

We must avoid letting the guest room become a sort of catch-all for cast off furniture, trinkets, and last season's clothes. There should be plenty of space in the closet to hang their garments and room for their shoes and suitcases. A clock helps the guests know what time it is when they awaken, and then they know whether to get up or wait awhile. A bedside table and lamp, dresser with a good mirror, a chair, wastebasket, box of tissue, and perhaps an extra light bulb (what if one burned out after the household had retired for the night?) are all essentials for a well-equipped guest room.

The guests' bathroom should have plenty of fresh towels, fresh soap, a drinking cup, and plenty of toilet tissue. We want to spare our guests from having to ask for anything that might embarrass them.

There are some other articles one might consider adding to her guest room, which can give her guests a sensation of pampered luxury and make them remember her as a gracious hostess. She may add a special touch by placing a scented candle and small box of matches on the dresser or bedside table (many people have a phobia of the electricity going off and being left in the dark in unfamiliar surroundings).

It is a pleasant touch to have the candle burning when guests arrive. It will create a warm feeling and a good fragrance in the room besides.

A vase of fresh flowers from the yard or local grocery store is inexpensive but adds so much atmosphere. A basket of fruit in the guest room serves a two-fold purpose. It is not only attractive but it also provides a snack if the guest is hungry.

An insulated water pitcher and glass, some good books and magazines, an iron and small ironing board, and a basket filled with items they might have forgotten but need, all make our guest's visit a pleasant experience. One can pick up little items in trial sizes to fill the basket with at most discount department stores such as: hair spray, toothbrush and toothpaste, deodorant, Band-Aids, feminine napkins, aspirin, antacid tablets, nail file, comb, razor, and shampoo. A perfectly equipped guest room combines all the comforts of a first-class hotel with the personal touches that only a considerate hostess can provide.

Because we do not have the staff a hotel restaurant has, we have to give special thought to plan our menus when we have guests that will be spending the night. We certainly want our guests to enjoy their meals, but we want to prepare things that do not cause us to live in the kitchen the duration of their stay. A woman can plan ahead casseroles that can be assembled ahead of time and popped into the oven with little effort. Grandma's fresh apple tarts may be super-delicious, but if a person has to spend three hours preparing them while her guests are sitting alone, it is not worth the effort. It would be better to choose a dessert that she could make ahead of time or utilize something simple.

Some people enjoy a big breakfast, while others cannot look an egg in the eye until afternoon, so we must check with our guests about what type of breakfast they prefer. We can let them know we are happy to prepare whatever they would enjoy most.

We should not require them to get up at any certain time to accommodate our family's routine. They are guests in our home, so we should allow them the luxury of a leisure time. If our family has early morning schedules to meet, we can go ahead and eat without the guests. We can have something light with our guests when they get up.

Perhaps all of this sounds frightening. We need not worry; we will not have overnight guests many times during the year—unless perhaps you are a minister's wife! Revivals and special services sometimes require the pastor's home to be a full-time hotel and restaurant. This can be very taxing on the pastor's wife, and an invitation to someone else's home for dinner can be a real break for her.

Entertaining the Minister and His Family

Many cartoons have portrayed the parishioner preparing a chicken dinner for the pastor, and much humor has accompanied the philosophy that eating chicken dinners is the main ministry of the pulpit! Ask any preacher's kid, and he will give you a very honest rebuttal to this misguided truth!

Many people feel uncomfortable having a minister in their home for dinner, and yet a minister is every bit as human when he sits down to a meal as they are. It is true that he is the anointed servant of God, yet there are no "big I's" or "little you's" in the kingdom of God. He will do everything possible to make the hostess feel comfortable while he is a guest in her home. The Lord has promised us a reward if we just give him a cup of cold water. Just think of the reward we will get for a whole meal!

The Shunammite woman learned how great the reward was for being hospitable to the prophet

Elisha. She went out of her way to provide a room so that Elisha would have a place to refresh himself when he passed through her town. Look at her reward! Her home that had never heard the pitter-patter of little feet was blessed with a son just as Elisha prophesied. When this son grew into manhood and fell ill in the field, it was Elisha's prayer that brought life back into his dead body. What a little investment this woman made to receive so much in return!

We may wonder what kind of home Mary and Martha had. Jesus seemed to enjoy going there often to visit. We notice their reward for entertaining Jesus—their brother, Lazarus, walked out of the family tomb after being dead four days! Martha was probably a perfectionist and worked especially hard to prepare for her guests. Mary, on the other hand, had the unique art of giving her guests her full attention.

Luke 10:38-42 tells us about one particular visit Jesus had at their home. Martha wanted Mary to help her serve and yet Mary was sitting listening to every word Jesus had to say. Jesus gave a very good piece of advice to the hostess. He reminded her that everything did not have to be perfect when she entertained. After the food is eaten it will be forgotten. However, if we will stop and enjoy our guests, we can glean so much from what they share with us through their conversation.

We can expose our family to the ministry. It will be an enriching experience not only for us but an investment to benefit our children. There is always a special closeness to be shared when we eat a meal together. Our children will feel closer to their pastor if he has been in their home. Many young people have expressed that when temptation came, they were able to resist only because they did not want to hurt their pastor, whom they felt was a close, caring friend. Many a young evangelist has influenced teens to live for God and stay in the church because they admired him and saw God in him outside the pulpit. When we share our home with the minister and his family, we reap many rewards.

When our church has special services and we would enjoy entertaining the visiting minister, it will make him feel more at ease if we will invite the pastor's family also. The visiting minister is actually a guest of the pastor while he is in our city, and it would be distasteful if we excluded either of them in our invitation.

Saying Good-bye

When our guests announce their intention of leaving, we should not urge them to stay. There is no harm in saying, "Oh, must you go?" in tones of disappointment if we feel that way, but we should not firmly refuse to let them depart or act offended that they are leaving so soon. Because people want to go home before we expect them to does not mean they have had a dull time. They may have something important to do the next day, or they may be tired for reasons we know nothing about. When they say they must go, we need to let them go as graciously as we welcomed them.

We also must not worry about any mistakes we might have made in being a hostess. When we have done our best, people appreciate us for it. We will probably even be surprised at the compliments we will hear in the following weeks about our hospitality.

Every hostess would like things to be perfect every time guests are present but nobody is perfect all the time. Julia Child's soufflé caves in sometimes!

A minister's wife recently had guests in her home for dinner. She had gone to great lengths to see that every detail was attended to because she considered her guests very important and quite scholarly in etiquette and social graces. In fact, the hostess had just attended a hospitality seminar taught by one of her guests.

The guests arrived earlier than expected, and the casserole in the oven was not quite done. The oven was turned up to speed up its progress and, of course, the inevitable happened—it burned. The humiliated hostess wanted to cry, but that would have only made matters worse, so very honestly, she briefly expressed her intentions for everything to be perfect, shared a laugh, scraped off the burnt part, and served it without mentioning it again. No amount of lamenting the fact that it was burned could have changed the situation, so she made the best of it and enjoyed her company.

Entertaining can be an experience of fun and fulfillment or dread and disaster. It all depends on our planning and organization. We do not have to be a queen or live in a palace to entertain successfully. God has made us women and given us a home. We need to do all we can do to see that we become the best hostesses we can possibly be and leave the rest up to Him.

Test Your Knowledge

1. Name three things Abraham did to make the angels that visited him feel welcome.
2. Why is it important to learn to be a good hostess to the unsaved?
3. What should our conversation center around when we have guests in our home?
4. Name at least ten essential items that a guest room needs.
5. Name at least ten items that will add a sense of luxury to the guest room.

6. What important principle do we need to remember when inviting a visiting minister to our home?

7. What important advice did Jesus give to Martha that we need to remember as well?

8. Name at least one reward for being hospitable to the ministry.

9. Does everything have to be perfect in order for our guests to enjoy their visit in our home?

10. Name two things God has given to us to help us become a gracious hostess.

Apply Your Knowledge

Begin today to plan a time when you will invite an unsaved friend over to your home for dinner. Ask for God's direction in who will respond to Him through your hospitality. Invite a new convert over for refreshments after service this week. Build a bond of friendship that will strengthen her in the church. Find out when the next special services are scheduled in your church. Let your pastor's wife know you want to open your home to help her entertain the visiting minister. Invite the youth group over for a simple snack and games. Watch God reward you for your efforts.

Expand Your Knowledge

Make a trip to your local library and check out several books on entertaining. Try some new table settings and recipes on your family to gain experience.

You and Your World 13

Whatsoever thy hand findeth to do, do it with thy might; for there is no work, nor device, nor knowledge, nor wisdom, in the grave, whither thou goest.

Ecclesiastes 9:10

> **Start with the Scriptures**
> Judges 4
> Ruth 1-4
> Esther 4:14
> Psalm 51:10-13; 139:14
> Matthew 21:19; 25:14-30
> I Corinthians 12:9-27
> Philippians 4:8, 11-13
> Colossians 2:10

God made each of us with strengths and weaknesses, likes and dislikes, abilities and inabilities. Each person has a distinct personality and a unique appearance. Out of five billion people, we are identified by a small fingerprint, a drop of blood, our voice inflections on a sound wave, or maybe even one hair from our head. Yet the greatest attributes God has given us are the ability to change or adapt, and the right and will to choose our state of mind.

Then why are some Christians discontented? We are discontented because we spend ourselves trying to change situations and circumstances which are out of our command. In Philippians 4:11, Paul said, "I have learned, in whatsoever state I am, therewith to be content." God has given us the authority and ability to change those things and areas of our lives of which we have charge. Then we must adjust or adapt.

Who Am I

If we are complete in Jesus, and we are, according to Colossians 2:10, then why do we have strengths and weaknesses? The answer is, "To complement others in the family of God." Using our abilities, we minister to others. Our inabilities allow others to minister to us. We need each other to be complete in the body of Christ. This is God's perfect plan. Frustration comes when we will not accept or admit our weaknesses as part of God's will for our lives.

We may sometimes find ourselves wanting to be like others. What we are saying is, "God, You did not do a good job of making me. You made me inferior to others." Therefore, jealous feelings arise. Jealousy breeds bitterness, and bitterness grows into vented anger. Then guilt becomes our silent partner. Contentment vanishes and we become competitive in the body of Christ.

In Helen Steiner Rice's poem, "Everything Is by Comparison," she compared only opposites. This is our nature. It takes the rain to make us appreciate the sunshine; it takes the darkness to make us appreciate the light. When we compare ourselves to others, we look at our own weaknesses and the others' strengths. If we did not have weaknesses, others could not have strengths.

In I Corinthians 12, Paul explained how spiritual gifts were dispersed to make up the church body.

Different gifts, administrations, operations, and manifestations were divided among the body, by God, as He pleased. We must realize who we are—a creation of God, individually designed for a purpose. In our place, we function well. Out of our place, we create a weakness (I Corinthians 12:27-31).

In Psalm 139:14, David said, "I am fearfully and wonderfully made: marvellous are thy works." God has endowed each of us with some talents (abilities), and a measure of faith to develop those talents.

Then where is our strength? In II Corinthians 12:9, Paul related the words of Jesus: "My strength is made perfect in weakness." In reality, is not this weakness subjection? Christ subjected Himself to the will of the Father and that became His strength. Of himself, Paul said, "For when I am weak, then am I strong" (II Corinthians 12:10). Paul paralleled himself to the pattern of Christ. Like Paul, our strength is in Christ, not in ourselves.

In the parable of the talents (Matthew 25:14-30), the master gave the talents according to each servant's ability. He also expected to reap according to each servant's ability. The one who hid his talent failed, not because of lack of ability but rather because of an improper evaluation of his master. He saw him as a hard man, partial and unfair, expecting something for nothing. Actually, the master gave much for little (verses 21 and 23).

When we compare our abilities to those of others and discover we have less, we falsely accuse God of partiality. We become bitter and bury the talents we have. The faithful servants each presented a different gain to the master according to their God-given talents. However, their rewards were the same, determined by faithfulness, not by gain.

Parable of the Talents
Matthew 25:14-30

- The talents *belonged* to the master.
- The master *gave* the talents out for a purpose.
- The master *expected* a return.
- *Equal rewards* were given because of the servants' faithfulness, regardless of their abilities.
- The talents *were not* the reward.

We must see talents as gifts from God for a purpose, to be returned to Him. The reward is not the talent. Our faithfulness in using the talent brings the reward. We are an instrument of God, created for a purpose—to glorify Him.

Where Am I?

In the poem, "Where Is the Sea?" by Felicia Hemans, the fish frantically searched for the sea as they swam the ocean blue. In their fervor, they did not realize where the ocean turned into the sea. In search of our world, we constantly change direction. Start! Stop! Start! Stop! Unfinished tasks, unreached goals. Each time we change courses, we lose momentum. Discouragement grows, incentive dies, depression sets in and a lack of self-worth results.

In Judges 4, two women became active in the Lord's army. Deborah, who had already attained public dignity as a judge of Israel, inspired the army of Israel to a great victory. However, in the same battle, it was an obscure woman, Jael, who actually killed Sisera, the leader of the enemy. Jael was used to fulfill the prophecy of Deborah: "For the Lord shall sell Sisera into the hand of a woman" (Judges 4:9).

Although Deborah gave all the credit to God, tribute is paid to Jael for putting Sisera to death. Neither woman is mentioned before Judges 4. Their availability brought them together from two positions of life to accomplish a task for the Lord.

In seeking greatness or searching for a ministry, we often find ourselves unavailable when an opportunity avails. We become lost in our own efforts to do something! Again, we are measuring with the wrong yardstick—the accomplishments of others.

Probably the most romantic story of the Bible was written in the Book of Ruth. Because of her loyalty and faithfulness, Ruth chose to glean the fields for survival. She chose to leave the comforts of home and the security of her own people. With no complaining, she went to work in the fields to provide for her mother-in-law and herself, believing that she would find grace in the sight of Boaz.

Ruth possibly knew which field to choose, that Boaz owned it, and that he was wealthy. All of this she may have known because of Naomi. God uses others to advise us. By following counsel, we find opportunities. The spirit of submission is the secret to blessing, especially when we are facing the unknown.

Ruth's desire was to find grace and favor in the sight of Boaz so that she and Naomi might survive. In her dedication to the task at hand, she was immediately noticed by Boaz, who showed her kindness and became her redeemer and husband. Ruth, the impoverished widow from Moab, became the great-grandmother of David because she understood and applied God's principles of submission.

By circumstance or providence, we, like Ruth, find opportunities in our own "world" to choose a field of labor, to know the owner (God), and to believe in His wealth (promises). If we seek to find favor and grace in the sight of God, He will show us kindness and make us profitable members of His kingdom. We should not seek talents or the rewards, but rather we should seek grace and favor in the sight of God. As Isaiah, we should say, "Here am I, Lord. Use me."

In "The Road Not Taken," by Robert Frost, the traveler took the road less traveled "because it was grassy and wanted wear." In conclusion, he said,

> "Two roads diverged in a wood, and I—
> I took the one less traveled by,
> And that has made all the difference."
>
> *Robert Frost (1875-1963)*

We should learn to be content on the road less traveled if that is the one we choose. Thanking God for peace and tranquility, we pray for those who must take the lead. We become good followers. God may someday need us to lead. And, in God's kingdom, one who has never learned to follow should never expect to lead.

Where Am I Going?

A sense of direction—where does it come from? The psychiatrist will often ask a disturbed person, "What do you want out of life?" The person will most often answer, "I don't know." This is not true with the happy person, for he will know. He may say, "Security, love and happiness," but he knows what he wants. The unhappy person looks at others and thinks, "They are happy because they have everything." In reality, contentment comes not from things possessed, but from a commitment to a cause, resulting in a clear sense of direction.

Even a hard day of work brings contentment if we know where we are going. Commitment to a goal lightens the routine of the task. It is believed that in body stress, a few minutes of worry or frustration is equal to hours of hard work. Loving what we are doing changes it from a job to a joy, from a task to a thrill.

We need to learn to set goals and work toward them. In the beginning, God gave us the pattern. In Genesis 1, God created man, first in thought, then in image, then God actually made man in Genesis 2:7. We would not think of baking a cake without a recipe. Yet we sometimes go from day to day with no goals, accomplishing little.

The most valuable earthly possession we have, time, is wasted by negligence. If we expect nothing, we will be sure to get it. It is better to set a goal and miss it than to never set it. As one writer said:

> We may not always reach our goals,
> But there is recompense in trying.
> Horizons broaden so much more,
> The higher we are flying.

Guidelines for Setting Goals

❶ Is it within my reach?

❷ Does it agree with the principles of God's Word?

❸ Does it allow harmony in my family?

❹ Will it glorify the kingdom of God?

❺ Is it worth working for?

We are not born with specific ambitions or goals. The people with whom we live and associate, family, friends, teachers and fellow workers mold our ambitions. We also are directed by personal desires that harmonize with our God-given talents. God will help us accomplish our goals, blending our desires and talents, if we commit ourselves to Him. "In all thy ways acknowledge him, and he shall direct thy paths" (Proverbs 3:6).

Suppose life brings hardships. What then? Joseph did not enjoy the hatred of his brothers. Neither did he aspire to be a ruler of Egypt. God chooses some for unusual works. It seems that He directs every phase of their lives. This road is not easy. And we, looking on, do not see the hardships involved. We want to be a ruling Joseph or a Queen

Esther without the cost of getting there. God will call, equip, and sustain some to special works.

> One ship drives east and another drives west,
> With the selfsame winds that blow.
> 'Tis the set of the sails and not the gales,
> Which tells us the way to go.
>
> *"Winds of Fate,"*
> *Ella Wheeler Wilcox*
> *(1850-1919)*

How Will I Go?

We are what we think, for as a woman thinketh in her heart, so is she (Proverbs 23:7). Our mind controls our body and God has given us the ability to choose our state of mind.

To accomplish our goals in life we must first learn to control our thinking process. Frustration, depression, anxiety, and worry are conditions of the mind that hinder our progress toward a fruitful life.

To control our thinking pattern we need to understand our own personality temperament. How do we react to the world around us? Why do we become angry when others laugh? How can one situation stimulate some and depress others?

In her books, *Personality Plus* and *Your Personality Tree*, Florence Littauer analyzes the basic personality types. What is normal behavior to one person can be abnormal behavior to another. However, God has given us the ability to control behavior—through our mind.

Understanding our personality does not give us license to be moody, rude, or unfriendly. It should help us control our mental state and live a happier and more fulfilled life. We need to accept the responsibility of our actions and to take control of our heart (mind).

Establish your heart. We must determine our goals now! What do we want out of life? If we want to be a faithful Christian, we must start today. If we want to be financially secure, we need to control spending. If we want to be healthy, then we need to eat healthful food, exercise, and keep a positive mental attitude. If we want to be happy, we should act happy, think happy thoughts. Smile! "Finally, brethren, whatsoever things are true . . . honest . . . just . . . pure . . . lovely . . . of good report . . . think on these things" (Philippians 4:8). The idle mind does not conceive (produce), does not reason, and is the devil's workshop.

"Keep thy heart with all diligence; for out of it are the issues of life" (Proverbs 4:23). We are responsible for our thoughts. We are to control them. Perhaps we could memorize and say to ourselves, "I may not be responsible for the actions of others, but I am responsible for the way I react to their actions."

The emotions of anger and resentment are destructive to the mind, body, and soul. Two other emotions which will stagnate our lives are loneliness and selfishness. We need to understand their makeup. Loneliness is being uncomfortable with oneself (low self-esteem). Selfishness is being uncomfortable with others (self-protection). We should refuse to allow emotions to control our heart. Instead, we can think, memorize verses of Scripture, and pray.

Organize our heart. We need to set our priorities and then allow them to guide us through each day. This will protect us from the guilt of neglect. There are twenty-four hours in a day—and we are one person. Time is a gift from God. We can conserve it and make it profitable.

Commit our heart:
- To God—a clean heart;
- To happiness—a right spirit.

"Create in me a clean heart, O God; and renew a right spirit within me. . . . Restore unto me the joy of thy salvation. . . . Then will I teach transgressors thy ways; and sinners shall be converted unto thee" (Psalm 51:10-13).

Share our heart. A person with a clean heart, a right spirit, and the joy of salvation will have something to share with others. A fruitful Christian is happy. In Matthew 21:19, Jesus cursed the barren fig tree. Then, it withered. An unfruitful Christian will spiritually wither.

Listen to our heart. Women need to be led by the Spirit of God. In the busy world we live in, we too often do not take time for meditation. How can we hear from God if we never listen? We can organize and discipline our lives so well that we leave the Spirit of God out.

It was not by chance that the Samaritan journeyed on the road to Jericho, felt compassion, and took time to show mercy toward the injured man. If we listen to the Spirit of God, He will open opportunities for our ministry. He will lead us to opportunities. "If we live in the Spirit, let us also walk in the Spirit" (Galatians 5:25).

When Will I Arrive?

If we love God and dedicate our lives to Him, we probably will never feel that we have "arrived" until we reach the heavenly city. However, there is a safe place in Christ that He provides for us to relax in and enjoy. This place can be called the "sanctuary of truth."

Webster's New World Dictionary states, "Truth is the state or quality of being in accordance with experience, facts, or reality." When our experience is real, based on the facts of the Bible, and our lives show the reality of the fruit of the Spirit, we are safe. Nothing can destroy truth.

On the road to Damascus, Paul faced truth, prompting him to ask, "Who art thou, Lord?" and "What wilt thou have me to do?" (Acts 9:5-6). Later, Paul was able to say, "I have learned to be content." Knowing the Lord and abiding by His commandments will give us a fruitful life and will bring contentment.

Life is full of mountains (struggles). As we climb to the top of our mountains, we can look back over the trail. We do not see the fullness of our own lives until we look back. What a joy to look over a successful life when one has not compromised truth. Paul said, "I have fought a good fight, I have finished my course, I have kept the faith: henceforth there is laid up for me a crown of righteousness, which the Lord, the righteous judge, shall give me at that day" (II Timothy 4:7-8). Paul had reached his place of safety even in the face of death. His life was totally committed to the "righteous judge."

Test Your Knowledge

1. In Philippians 4:11, Paul said he had learned to _____ _____.

2. According to Colossians 2:10, you are _____ _____ in ____ _____.

3. We have strengths and weaknesses to _____ _____ others in the _____ of _____.

4. In II Corinthians 12:10, Paul said, "For when I am _____, then am I _____."

5. In the parable of the talents, the master gave out the talents according to _____ _____ _____ and the rewards were given according to the servant's _____.

6. The idle mind does not _____, does not _____ and is the _____'s workshop.

7. Refuse to allow your _____ to control your heart.

8. _____ is being uncomfortable with yourself. _____ is being uncomfortable with others.

9. In Matthew 21:19, Jesus _____ the barren fig tree. An unfruitful Christian will spiritually _____.

10. Knowing _____ and abiding by _____ will give us a fruitful life and will bring contentment.

Apply Your Knowledge

Carefully study the material presented in this chapter and apply it to your life. Endeavor to live a contented, purposeful life that is productive for the kingdom of God.

Expand Your Knowledge

To understand God's plan for your life, get the *More to Life* Bible study—three books with four lessons each. Also, consider *The Good Life* for young girls, and *Notable Women of Scripture* by Ken Gurley. These books are available through the Pentecostal Publishing House, 8855 Dunn Road, Hazelwood, MO 63042-2299 (*www.pentecostalpublishing.com* and 866-819-7667).

Other good resources include *Emotions, Can You Trust Them?* by Dr. James Dobson, and *Personality Plus* and *Your Personality Tree*, both by Florence Littauer.

PGSTL